YEARS

**SIMON &
SCHUSTER
PAPERBACKS**

THE
SHIFT

CHANGE YOUR PERSPECTIVE,
NOT YOURSELF

TINX

SIMON & SCHUSTER PAPERBACKS

NEW YORK LONDON TORONTO SYDNEY NEW DELHI

100 YEARS
SIMON &
SCHUSTER
PAPERBACKS

An Imprint of Simon & Schuster, LLC
1230 Avenue of the Americas
New York, NY 10020

First Simon & Schuster trade paperback edition May 2024

SIMON & SCHUSTER PAPERBACKS and colophon are registered trademarks of Simon & Schuster, LLC

Simon & Schuster: Celebrating 100 Years of Publishing in 2024

For information about special discounts for bulk purchases, please contact Simon & Schuster Special Sales at 1-866-506-1949 or business@simonandschuster.com.

The Simon & Schuster Speakers Bureau can bring authors to your l ive event. For more information or to book an event, contact the Simon & Schuster Speakers Bureau at 1-866-248-3049 or visit our website at www.simonspeakers.com.

Interior design by Carly Loman

Manufactured in the United States of America

10 9 8 7 6 5 4 3 2 1

Library of Congress Cataloging-in-Publication Data has been applied for.

ISBN 978-1-6680-0763-1
ISBN 978-1-6680-0764-8 (pbk)
ISBN 978-1-6680-0765-5 (ebook)

To my girls: Do no harm. And take no shit.

"Above all, be the heroine of your life, not the victim."

—Nora Ephron

CONTENTS

PART 2:

TOGETHER AND APART

(COUPLING UP, BREAKING UP, AND GETTING OVER IT)

PART 3:

SELF-WORTH AND SELF-KNOWLEDGE

(THE ERA OF SELF-DISCOVERY)

INTRODUCTION

Not to be that basic bitch who starts her book with a *Sex and the City* analogy, but . . . we need to discuss the fact that the central crisis in that iconic show boiled down to Big vs. Aidan. A series that included four successful, independent women (okay, Carrie's autonomy is debatable) with thriving careers, phenomenal wardrobes, and, most important, rock-solid friendships, came down to: Will she end up with this guy or that guy? (Or ballet guy, but let's be real, he was never really in the running.) We all know that Carrie was incredibly narcissistic, which is why it's so ironic that such a self-centered person focused solely on whom she was or wasn't attached to. The fact is, she put all her worth in the hands of those men, and we ate it up. Doesn't matter whether you were Team Big or Team Aidan, there was no concern about Carrie becoming her best self or discovering her own happiness—the only thing that mattered was whom she ended up with. *I couldn't help but wonder* . . . is that what women do?

We spend so much time and effort trying to find someone to make us feel whole and valid, never asking "Who makes me feel most like myself?" or "What do I even like?" *We waste precious years of our lives looking outward during the time we should be looking inward to figure out exactly who we really are and exactly what we really need.* By the time we do enter into a relationship, that sense of self and those wants and needs are so obscured, they get consumed by the wants and needs of others. And that's why so many women end up sad and unhappy later in life. In the pursuit of finding someone to share their lives with, they gave themselves up.

As women, we need to be laser focused on what makes us feel fulfilled and happy. The key to this is something I call The Shift. Think of it like rewiring the neural pathways in your brain and replacing old patterns that don't serve you with new ones that do. *The Shift is a simple way to slightly change your thinking and flip the unempowering scripts that so many of us fall prey to.* Me included.

I'm Tinx and if I'm not already serving as your agony aunt on the internet and/or radio, let me tell you that my main mission in life is to help other women know their self-worth. I suppose how and why I got here deserves a little explanation, so here we go.

I was born in DC to American parents and moved to England as a baby. I grew up in London and went to an all-girls school, which was the single most influential factor in my formative years, the through line of everything that's come since.

Being surrounded by women has always grounded me, and I think the bonds between women are tighter than any connection on the planet. If you'll allow me to get a little woo-woo for a moment, I truly believe there's a deeper level to sisterhood and solidarity, something that binds women together on a biological, spiritual, and existential level. The complexities of the female experience feel like part of a larger common experience—and I don't think men feel the same way. Something about being a woman is cosmic and so fucking cool. I always felt really tapped into that, even as a young girl.

Don't get me wrong—I LOVE men. I love to flirt. I love sex. But I will forever be hoes before bros. If I see a hot guy, I might trail off in conversation a bit, but I always come back to my team. And that's because I spent such a crucial part of my life focused only on girlfriends, with guys as an extracurricular. Like Cher said, men are just dessert.

Then I went to college, and all that went out the window. It was like I had grown up on a strict diet and then suddenly went to an all-you-can-eat buffet. It was extremely exciting, and to go with this whole buffet metaphor, I gained my freshman fifteen and then some. Boys had been an after-school treat, but now they lived directly across the hallway from me—it was fresh, hot college guys for breakfast, lunch, and dinner.

I learned a lot in the decade that followed: namely, how to not lose yourself in the pursuit of a guy who doesn't value you, which would evolve into one of my most renowned dating concepts: Box Theory (more on that later). I learned that I felt better when I focused inward, and also when I surrounded myself with other women. I learned that I was happiest when writing, so I started freelancing pieces where I threw myself into crazy situations, like going on a date every week for a year, or hooking up with my trainer. I loved slipping on the banana peel so others could learn from my mistakes. I also learned that just because you love writing and fashion does not mean you will be happy going to grad school for it in New York, where I ended up watching the entire anthology of *Real Housewives* and drinking a lot (a lot a lot) of wine.

I knew I needed a change, and Southern California had always intrigued me (I blame growing up watching *The Hills* and *Laguna Beach*), so I followed my curiosity, packed two suitcases, and moved to LA on my twenty-ninth birthday. I had no clue what I was going to do. I applied to work at a mustard company. ("I can work at a mustard company! I LOVE mustard!") My friends were getting married and working super-successful jobs, and I was settling for living in a dark, depressing studio above a strip club and working as a marketing consultant for a weed company, where I admitted to a bunch of pot professionals that I didn't know the difference between indica and sativa.

Nevertheless, there was a fire burning in me. I knew I needed to keep searching. Little by little, I took on more consulting clients, kept freelancing, made some friends, and started to feel the vibe in LA.

And then the pandemic hit.

I was still living in that sad, dark apartment and was so alone, so far from family. (Moment of self-awareness here: I had it much better than many, many people around the world. Don't cry for me, Quarantina.) All the consulting clients I had worked so hard to get were going bankrupt one by one. I was desperate to write, but shockingly no one was in the mood for lighthearted articles about leggings.

With the exception of an online controversy that would strip me to the bones a few years down the line (I believe this is what they call "foreshadowing" in the literary world?), it was the most confusing, most destabilizing time in my life, and my daily lifestyle and decisions reflected it.

It was about this time that I heard from friends about a new app that everyone was obsessed with in quarantine. It sounded like everyone was just learning the same dances to the same songs. "Weird," I thought. But also, what did I have to lose?

I made my first (dance-free) TikTok on May 1, 2020, and the rest is history.

Not to be dramatic, but I knew the moment I hit record that this was what I was put on earth to do. And everything in my life had, strangely, prepared me for it. Going to an all-girls school, being president of my sorority, living and dating in different cities, and constantly throwing myself into wild situations had all trained me to help other women through tricky circumstances, especially when it came to dating. I definitely never pretended to have all the answers, and regularly prove that to this day. But I think if something I say can help someone skip over weeks wasted worrying about a guy, then I'm living my life's purpose.

Some might wonder what qualifies me to give advice when (a) I'm only thirty-two, which is old for TikTok but pretty young for seasoned wisdom, and (b) I've spent most of my time in the internet spotlight as a single person. Which brings me back to the *Sex and the City* conundrum—what makes being part of a couple the most important qualification? Why is *that* the bar we measure everything against?

If you take away one thing from this book, let it be this: Dating is not a means to an end. The goal of dating is not to end up in a relationship. The goal is to know yourself, completely. And by that metric, I'm wise as fuck. I've spent so much time falling on my face but then getting up and using each face-plant to learn more about who I am, what makes me happy, and what doesn't serve me. And over a lifetime of listening to other women's trials and tribulations when it comes to dating, I've observed that most of us are looking at it all wrong.

Let's imagine that dating is like playing a video game (stay with me here, I don't play video games either). Most people think the objective is to get to the end without falling off a cliff, getting squashed, or being clobbered by a huge evil toad. That's wrong. You're going to get scrapes and bruises along the way. You're going to go on bad dates. You're going to have your heart broken. *The point is not to get to the end unscathed. The point is to know yourself, discover what you like and don't like, and not let the destination overpower the journey.*

Once you stop thinking about dating as a means to an end and start thinking about it as an era of self-discovery, it changes everything. Which brings me to The Shift. In a nutshell, The Shift is something you can do in any situation where your brain is looking for external validation. For example, if you're mentally spiraling over some dude and worrying, "Does he like me?" you can shift your thinking to "Do I like him?" or "How does he make me feel?" or "Actually, how's his dick game?" It reframes the inner narrative and reminds you that *you* are the prize.

Let's say you get home from a date and are going over it in your mind. Instead of thinking, "Is he gonna call me tomorrow?" you can shift the thought to "What did I learn about myself?" If it feels like an absurd question to ask yourself, that just proves how brainwashed we all are into this warped perception of what's considered a successful date. We *need* these paradigm shifts to undo the ingrained ways of thinking that push aside our own wants and needs in the name of pleasing others. Rewiring your brain takes effort, but aren't you worth it?!

When you incorporate The Shift into your life, your whole energy changes. Instead of feeling like you are at the mercy of the dating gods, you use dating as a tool for personal growth that fuels you instead of fatigues you. It helps simplify decision-making and puts the power back in your hands. Which, wouldn't you know it, makes you way hotter and helps your dating game in the process.

In this book, I'll give you various shifts, theories, and "holy fucking shit" breakthroughs you can apply to your life on a daily basis. We will cover everything from texting to hooking up to breakups to taking better care of yourself. I'll share stories from my own misadventures, as well as tips and tricks I've learned along the way.

HUGE disclaimer: I am giving advice and sharing observations from my perspective, which is that of a privileged, straight, cisgendered woman. I would never want to speak from an unqualified place, and thus, I focus on dating dynamics between heterosexual men and women. There are so many brilliant books about LGBTQ+ relationships, so I'm staying in my extremely straight lane and writing what I know. However, my main message comes down to self-worth and prioritizing your own happiness, so if that's something you think you'd like more of in your life, you are welcome here!

That said, if you picked up this book hoping to unlock the secret to snagging a husband, this is probably not the book for you. I acknowledge and appreciate that there are so many different schools of thought and reasons to date, so I'm not knocking the ring seekers. But if your main goal in life is to be half of a pair, then you might want to look elsewhere, because this book is about finding self-fulfillment above all else.

Other things this book is not: a "survival guide" (dating is not something to endure or be on the defense about—it should be a fun, enlightening time) or a man-hating tantrum (you can adore men—as I do—and want to get married—as I do—but you don't need to sacrifice any part of yourself to do so).

Just remember: this is not a win-lose, pass-fail situation. *Dating is not just what you do until you link up with someone and live happily ever after.* If you do it right, it's a period of introspection, a time of self-exploration, and an era of your life you will protect fiercely and look back on fondly.

Knowing that . . . welcome to *The Shift*, sister. Grab a drink and let's get into it.

PART 1

DATING

(CRUSHES, TEXTING, FIRST DATES, AND HOOKING UP)

SCARCITY MINDSET:

HER SUCCESS IS NOT MY FAILURE

"We raise girls to see each other as competitors
not for jobs or accomplishments, which I think can
be a good thing, but for the attention of men."

—Chimamanda Ngozi Adichie, *We Should All Be Feminists*

Before we get into the nitty-gritty, we gotta get our heads right. Because *The Shift* is all about analyzing your thought process and making it work for you instead of against you. And the number one thing that holds women back in this department is a scarcity mindset.

From birth, all of us are conditioned to view the world in terms of limited resources: there are limited jobs for women; good men are so hard to find; there's only one "hot girl" in any given setting. Now, obviously there is a hint of truth to some of this, as far as opportunities for women. But let me tell you something: There are plenty, *plenty* of great men. A good man being some needle in the haystack is just a lie that's fed to us to keep us in line. And if another girl gets a wonderful guy, she isn't taking that opportunity from you.

One of my favorite sayings is "Her success is not my failure." It's something we need to drill into our heads every day, because the world is all too willing to tell us the opposite. And having a scarcity mindset makes us move through the world in a fear-based state, approaching every potential relationship as a loaded opportunity to secure your spot. It makes you think "I need to make him like me" before you've even figured out whether you like him. It's why we get so upset when someone ghosts us or ends a relationship—we think we've lost our last chance.

> **THE SHIFT:** I want what she has ➝ There's enough to go around, and I'll find what's meant for me

I want to help you let this mindset go, but I know it requires a big perspective makeover. So let's play a little visualization game. Imagine if I told you that in one year from now, you're going to be engaged to the man of your dreams, and you're going to be happier than you've ever been. Knowing that, how would you act in the meantime? You'd probably enjoy your current situation more, taking advantage of this special time that's just yours, right? So LIVE THAT WAY NOW. *Act as though your dream life is on the horizon and you've got to make the most of what's in front of you today.* Because that's true! The sooner you let go of a scarcity mindset, the freer you are to make space for what's coming. It speeds up the process too—the more you have fun with friends, the more you invest in your career and family, the more you use this time for self-exploration, the more you put out the kind of energy that will attract what you're eventually looking for in a partner. Most important, you become your best self and we love her!

> **THE SHIFT:** I really want to find someone ➝ I know I will

I wasted so much time in my twenties worrying that I'd never find my match. But now I act as though it's already happened, because chances are, it will. Think about it: Humans have been falling in love since the dawn of civilization. Do you think you're the rare person who is never going to find love? Chances are you'll end up with someone. It would actually be harder to avoid meeting a mate your entire life. So let's just assume you'll find someone. And when you do, you don't want to look back and think, why did I waste the last year of my singlehood being a miserable sop instead of having fun?

That's the gift of an abundance mindset—it reframes the way you look at being single so that you can savor this time. Instead of being sad to wake up alone, you starfish in your bed and appreciate the solitude. It doesn't feel lonely when you know that in the future you'll have to get up at five in the morning and take care of a baby or that you'll have a stinky snoring man next to you. It gives you the courage to take that spontaneous solo trip or pursue that random passion because soon enough you might not be in the same place in life and that's okay. But for now, every moment is precious. Because it really is.

CRUSH LIST:

PART MANIFESTATION, PART ORGANIZATION, MAGIC SPELL-MEETS-SPREADSHEET

"Thoughts become things."

—Rhonda Byrne, *The Secret*

I've read approximately a million books about women and yet have never really come across another book (or podcast or even interview) that zeroes in on the power inherent in being a young woman. Teenage girls and their passions are trivialized and mocked, but the truth is that there's something incredibly potent in that energy. I mean, I pretty much owe my entire career to a platform fueled by young girls dancing, sharing their love for books, and being creative. And if I had to think of one thing that perfectly encapsulates tween girl magic, it's a crush.

"Crush" is one of my favorite words in the English language. It makes me think of the color pink. It makes me feel like eating candy. It makes me want to listen to nineties pop songs. And I think it's vastly underused. People think that crushes are frivolous and silly, but I am one hundred percent powered by them on a day-to-day basis. Allow me to explain.

We've been told that crushes are reserved for middle school kids. And that's exactly why I intentionally use the word. There's a purity to crushes that infuses them with an almost witchy magic. Crushes are about the possibility of what could be. They're based in imagination, hope, and optimism. We have a crush on our favorite singer when we're fourteen and we go to his concert thinking that he might see us in the crowd and it'll be love at first sight. Can you even handle the absolute audaciousness?! Then suddenly we turn twenty-one and are working our first job and there's a switch that happens where we lose that hallucinatory imagination and instead put all our efforts into dressing and acting for a guy at the office who doesn't even give us butterflies. As adults, we often go from kinda liking someone to dating them and then all of a sudden it's super serious and we've skipped over all the fun. *The time before things become real is supercharged with possibility— and you can't get that time back once things progress.* Pre-dating should be a whimsical part of your life where you can fully revel in that excitement and really absorb it.

But how? We need to shift our minds back to that time when we were free with our infatuation, when we crushed HARD without fear. Which brings me to the crush list—a genius concept introduced to me by my friend Livvie. This is a powerful practice that is part manifestation, part organization. Kind of like a vision board meets fantasy football draft (from what I understand of that). And it's one of the most healthy and helpful things you can do for yourself.

Here's how it works: A crush list is kept in your phone—I recommend starting a list in your Notes app labeled "groceries," "packing list for girls' trip," "leg workout," or something similarly boring. Now, anytime you have a little tingle for a guy, you add him to the list. This includes people you know, friends of friends, old flames, or that cute guy you see once a week at the coffee shop, but it can also be a celebrity or some-one you've never met. (By the way, I've put several celebrities on my crush list and they've been called into my life. Your mileage may vary, especially if you do not live in LA, attend parties every night, and post every moment of your life on so-cial media. All I'm saying is, trust the power.)

Once you've added someone to your crush list, it's like you've put a little message in a bottle and sent it out to sea. You've given the crush power, released it out into the world, and now Jesus/the Universe/fate can take the wheel.

Are you still hung up on the previous paragraph and won-dering what celebs I put crush list spells on? Well, I won't name names, but I will say there have been three so far.

A Tale of the Crush List in Three Musical Acts:

Act 1: Once upon a time there was a hot DJ whom I put on the crush list, and through the powers that be, I ended up on a date with him. I literally vlogged the whole thing so if you're truly curious about who it was, this one's not a hard case to crack.

Act 2: I read an interview with a very famous musician and realized how smart he was and thought we'd have a good conversation. I added him to the crush list and then went about my life not thinking anything of it. Wouldn't you know it, he started following me on Instagram. And we went on a few dates! Hopefully he doesn't read this because he doesn't need any help with his ego.

Act 3: I had added another male music act to the crush list (I guess I have a type—you know what they say: those who can't sing fuck those who can). In any case, we ended up DMing and he happened to be in Vegas the same night I was there for my birthday. What happens in Vegas stays in Vegas, but let's just say I went from crushing to smashing and it was a happy birthday indeed.

Now, am I saying that if you add Michael B. Jordan to your crush list that he will appear on your doorstep the next day? Hate to break it to you, but my crush list alchemy has only resulted in some celeb-ish hookups because I live in LA and am celeb-adjacent with access to a huge pool of well-known and usually self-absorbed guys in the entertainment industry. I still recommend putting celebs and pie-in-the-sky pipe dream crushes on the list, but you also want to have some more Joe Schmos on there who intersect your daily life already.

I find that the most effective way to utilize the crush list in real life is if your friend says, "Oh there's this guy you might like who's coming to the party next weekend," then you put him on the list and pull that energy into your life. Or perhaps your sister sends you a photo of your niece's first-grade class and you see that the teacher is super fucking hot. Now Mr. Fletcher is on your list and the cosmos have taken note.

The best thing about crush lists is that they evolve with you. You can always add or subtract from your list. I like to do a big overhaul when the seasons change. You can take guys off the list who don't deserve their spot anymore. You can put new guys on the list who have popped into your mind during your last visit with your vibrator. Crush lists are also a great tool for better understanding what you're looking for in a guy. Analyzing your list from a perspective of "what does this say about me?" helps you identify the traits you really want—confidence, ambition, sensitivity, etc. Even if (or especially when) you're not in a relationship, you can discover your likes and dislikes and how they change over time. Then anytime you're feeling like, blah, I'm not seeing anyone right now, you can look at your crush list and say, there are so many people out there for me to meet.

> **THE SHIFT:** I'm not dating anyone ⟶ I'm crushing on Gym Guy so hard!

A note for all of you who start a crush list and then couple up and wonder what your boyfriend will do if he stumbles upon proof of you lusting after a bunch of other guys: Personally, I think it's okay to maintain your crush list, but see note above about naming it something inconspicuous. Keeping it on the back burner does not mean you are cheating. You can consciously put the crush list on pause, tell yourself you don't need to look at it, and just file it away with your old passwords, confirmation numbers, and list of future baby names.

For those of you ready to start actively manifesting, have fun with it! And remember, this isn't about a realistic assessment of dating prospects. Don't add all your matches on Hinge to your crush list. This is more for romanticizing your life. Gamifying things a bit. Lightening the mood. It's also just fun to add someone to the list and remind yourself that there's so much out there and that the universe is a totally magical place. (Me: does mushrooms once . . .) In all seriousness, it's about having an abundance mindset (see previous chapter) and enjoying some goddamn levity, okay?

I know we've all been beaten down by the responsibilities of adulthood, so just try to channel a time before you had to worry about taxes or rolling over your 401(k). Go back to when you were in middle school cutting up magazines to make collages for your room (um, hello, early vision boarding). Use your crush list as a tool to take things less seriously. Live, laugh, list.

BEFORE THE FIRST MESSAGE:

DATING APPS, DMS, AND THE ART OF ONLINE STALKING

"The odd thing about this form of communication is that you're
more likely to talk about nothing than something."

–Kathleen Kelly, *You've Got Mail*

I know we just talked about crush lists and living in a romantic
dream world, but to bring it back to earth for a sec, let's acknowledge the fact that it's probably more likely that you'll meet
a dating prospect through your phone than in line at the grocery
store or, even the old classic, at a bar. As much as I'd like to live
in a world where we meet our soulmates by bumping into them
at a bookstore, swiping your way to a date is just the way of
the world now. With that said, let's clarify the purpose of apps.

DATING APPS ARE A TOOL, NOT AN ACTIVITY

Dating apps offer a key to a pool of options, a place where you
can browse to find someone you want to connect with in real
life—not a place where you spend time writing to your new pen
pal. They are about *access*, not engagement. Get in and get out,
girlfriend. Don't put the app in the "Social Media" group on
your phone. Group it with OpenTable, Yelp, and Uber—services
you use to find what you want to do in the actual world.

Now, I won't spend too much time on the art of dissecting dating app profiles, because we all know the architecture of every guy's Tinder: one photo of a past Halloween costume to show that they are funny and goofy, one photo of him doing something athletic to show that he's sporty and fit, one photo of him in a suit at a wedding because it shows that he's a grown-up. Perhaps a photo of him holding a child with the caption "NOT MINE!"

Point is, don't expect to be blown away by anyone's use of the interface. A short, witty headline and the absence of a bathroom selfie is really enough for us to work with. Once you find someone who makes you stop mindlessly swiping and go "hmmmm . . . ," then the important thing to keep in mind communication-wise is quality over quantity. Regardless of who reaches out first, try to move past the generic openers and get into a fun but pointed conversation as soon as possible. Any questions you ask should be no more than three degrees of separation from making plans. For example:

Is that the Fox Theatre? → Have you ever been to Cafe Van Kleef down the street from there? → They make a great greyhound. We should get drinks there this weekend ;)

Just remember, the guy on the other end of the dating app could be killing time while bored at work. But you are not *Candy Crush*! Stay focused, queen.

DM DOS AND DON'TS

I would be remiss not to address the now Boomer-appropriated "sliding into someone's DMs" on Instagram/TikTok/Snapchat/ whatever. I'm an advocate of this method and highly endorse being ballsy and going for it. *As the saying goes, life is not a dress rehearsal—this is the main performance.* However, there are some best practices to follow when doing the slide (cha-cha real smooth). I've given examples of good and bad messages that illustrate each concept because yes, I am your guardian angel!

1. BE FUNNY. This is the *most* important thing. You need to open with something that will grab their attention, especially since typically only the first sentence is visible before opening the message.

For example:

Bad: What are you looking for in a relationship? [Who are you, a father asking, "What are your intentions?" Save the seriousness for when you're three drinks in at the bar discussing reincarnation.]

Good: What's your Uber rating? [This is my opener and let's just say it has never disappointed.]

2. DON'T SAY "JUST" OR "I THINK." These water down your message and don't give off bad-bitch energy.

For example:

Bad: I think you're hot. Just wondering if you'd like to meet for drinks sometime?

Good: You're hot. Want to meet for drinks sometime? [Option 2 is stealing your man every time.]

3. BE CONFIDENT. This is the only surefire way to appear attractive when you're shooting your shot with an obscure profile pic and a username you picked in 2012. Your vibe should imply that this dude is lucky beyond belief that you've chosen him. This is not the time to be self-deprecating or apologetic.

For example:

Bad: Hi :) I came across your profile and you just have an amazing smile. I think we would get along—I'd love to get drinks sometime soon if you're open to it? PS this is my first ever DM slide, I hope this is flattering and not weird. I'm normal, I promise.

Good: Hey, I came across your profile and you have the best smile. I have a feeling we would get along. I'd love to get drinks with you sometime soon. PS this is my first ever DM slide. You should be flattered :) xx

4. BE BRIEF AND TAKE IT OFF THE APP. Unlike dating in general, which should not be goal-oriented, dating apps and DMs are there for a singular purpose: to help you meet someone in real life. He should not be planning dates through DM. His sending you memes on Instagram doesn't count as communication. (Disclaimer: If you're under twenty, this may be different.) Don't spend all your energy or waste all your wit in the inbox—save it for the date. And for the record, his watching your stories doesn't mean anything, besides maybe showing that he's bored. (Doesn't mean you can't put on a show for him in your stories and do a little thirst trapping, but don't put any real stock in the fact that he's seeing your posts—so is your childhood friend from camp, your sister-in-law, and your old co-worker.)

SO I CREEP, YEAH

Finally, we must address the understandable evil that comes along with shopping online for boyfriends: you inevitably do a little stalking. I'm not going to lie and pretend I'm above it, but I will say I think we should all try to avoid it, and not just because of the universal experience of accidentally liking a stranger's photo from sixty-two weeks ago.

I used to stalk the shit out of anyone I was going on a date with, but nowadays I really try to go into it blind, because I've found that every time I've met someone whom I had already done some research on, they always ended up being very different from whatever online presence they had. So I'd rather just get the accurate first impression in person. I also find that as a people pleaser, I'm less likely to morph myself into someone I think they will like if I haven't already discovered that they are a Rams fan and studied abroad in Prague. Instead, I'm able to be the real me, and meet the real them, and we go from there. I have honestly never seen any good come out of doing reconnaissance on a dating prospect.

Because here's the real trap: Instagram stalking before the first date or in the early stages messes with your ability to accurately assess the person. When you see photos with absolutely no context you're like, "Oh God, his ex was really pretty, he seems super sophisticated, looks like he parties a lot," etc. etc. Meanwhile his ex might have been a nightmare, he likes reenacting *Dumb and Dumber* with his buddies, and he enjoys curling up with a good book on Friday nights more than going out. The damaging thing here is that you start to form an image that is not based on reality. You think you're collecting real data, but all you've done is muddy the waters.

This can backfire in so many ways, including:

- making you more nervous for the first date than you should be
- putting the guy on a pedestal he hasn't earned (see Reverse Box Theory, page 25)
- trying to casually work what you've seen into the conversation without revealing that you've stalked (e.g., mentioning a concert you know they went to), which is not subtle at all and doesn't actually make the other person like you more

THE SHIFT: A little research doesn't hurt ⟶ What matters is how they make you feel

BEFORE THE FIRST DATE:

A COURSE IN BOX THEORY

"If he likes you, you'll know."

—Tinx Original

Okay, besties, it's time to get to the crown jewel of my dating advice. If I was to get a PhD, this would be my thesis. If I was to give a Ted Talk, this would be my topic. If I was to run for office, this would be my platform. Gather round for my magnum opus.

The gist of Box Theory is that when a guy meets you (in a romantic sense—we're not talking about family members, coworkers, or friends), he puts you in one of three boxes:

1. He wants to date you.
2. He wants to sleep with you.
3. He wants nothing to do with you.

Once he's made his selection, it is locked in. Listen up because this is important: YOU CANNOT SHIFT FROM BOX TO BOX. Women can meet a guy and think, "Oh, he seems fun for a quick fling," but then develop feelings for him and want to date him. We all have a friend who's like "omg I hooked up with my dorky optometrist lol how random" and then a month later they're engaged. What a woman wants out of a man can change based on circumstances and the way things organically evolve.

HOWEVER! Men do not (okay, devil's advocates, *very rarely*) switch the box they've put a woman in, and they come to their box selection almost independently of any tangible factors. The same woman might be dating-box material for one guy, hookup-box content for another, and "no thank you" for a third—all on the same day and even if she acts the exact same way with each of them. The point is, there is very little you can do to influence their choice—things that would normally be turnoffs they will find endearing, and conversely, trying to be what you think they want will not change their mind.

My first brush with Box Theory was in high school, when I got drunk and threw up on a guy's shoes and the next day he asked me to be his girlfriend. I was clearly in the dating box regardless of barf. Then in college, I pined over a water polo player named Jim who—despite my greatest efforts—tossed me in the hookup box quicker than he threw his ripped Speedos into the locker room trash. I began to sense a pattern. Over the next decade, I collected more data and solidified my theory.

In my studies, I discovered that guys don't really play games in two (very different) cases:

- they really like you
- they don't care about you at all

If he likes you, you'll know. He will ask you on a date far in advance. He will remember that your mom was getting foot surgery and ask how it went. He will show initiative (not just texting but following through).

Likewise, if he isn't interested, you'll also know (unless you are trying to convince yourself otherwise). He will respond to texts passively, never ask you questions, and no matter how hard you try, you won't be able to bring him around. The walls of the box are too high to climb.

If a guy puts you in the dating box, almost nothing you do will change his mind, including sleeping with him on the first date. Contrary to what so many of us think, giving it up on night one does not make a guy lose respect for you, instantly going from "Would my mom like her?" to "Never mind, looks like I'll only be calling her after ten p.m." And on the flip side, if a guy only wants to sleep with you, you could make him wait three months to smash and he still wouldn't change his mind from "bang her" to "marry her."

This is hugely liberating. Instead of worrying whether you should arbitrarily hold out until the third, fourth, or fifth date if you really like a guy, *just sleep with him when you want to.* Crazy, right?

THE SHIFT: How does he feel about me? → How does he make me feel?

So many girls get in their heads about a new guy without checking in with their bodies. You should register how he *physically* makes you feel. Not just when you're with him either. If you find yourself constantly checking your phone and you feel an anxiety you haven't felt since you took the SATs, that doesn't scream dating box. You *should* feel a buzzy, slightly nervous excitement, but there's a layer of calm underneath it—a sense of security, not frenzy and uncertainty.

Whenever you feel up in the air, just go back to how he makes you feel, and what his actions (not his words) show. But when in doubt, here's a cheat sheet:

SIGNS YOU'RE IN THE DATING BOX:

- He asks you on Monday to make plans for that weekend.
- He tries to extend the hangout when you're together.
- He remembers your friends' names.
- He takes a photo of you.
- He texts you just to check in—not only when making plans.
- He double texts (doesn't wait for you to volley the ball back to him).

SIGNS YOU'RE IN THE HOOKUP BOX:*

- He only texts you on the weekends.
- He says things like "What're your plans?" or "When am I seeing you?" (Passive bullshit—see "When We Hanging?" page 35.)

---

* Important note: Being in the hookup box is not always a bad thing! If you only want a hookup yourself, then rejoice in the mutual understanding. However, if you are hoping for a relationship and sleep with him because you want to get closer, but then he ghosts you, please understand he didn't change his mind about you because you hooked up with him. You were always in the hookup box and now you know. Rewrite the narrative and say, "I had fun and now he is dead to me." Hold a funeral (see page 91), get a pedicure, call a friend, and move on to the next.

- He says "You have a sister, right?" when you've told him you have three brothers you are very close to.
- He doesn't reach out to you the day after you've slept together.

SIGNS YOU'RE IN THE JUST-FRIENDS BOX:

- He never initiates plans and doesn't follow up after seeing you.
- Talking to him feels like a job interview: "Where did you go to college?" "How long have you lived on the West Coast?"
- He gives you a side hug.

Before I get off my soapbox (no pun intended), let me address the controversy surrounding this concept. Some Box Theory Deniers like to say that this mentality puts all the power in the guys' hands. And I have to disagree. Box Theory is all about taking back the power and making informed decisions based not on some mystical alchemy but, rather, *what you want.* In order to do that, you need to change the power dynamic—which brings me to my next theory . . .

REVERSE BOX THEORY:
EVIDENCE-BASED THINKING VS. FUTURE TRIPPING

> "I did something kind of wacky. I used Photoshop at
> work today to composite our faces together to see
> what our kids would look like. Our family album!"
>
> **–Andie Anderson,** *How to Lose a Guy in 10 Days*

I spent most of my twenties being obsessed with complete los-
ers. For the sake of our research, we will name all of them
Chris. Chris wore short-sleeve button-downs, worked some
unremarkable job at a big tech company, and lived with four
other Chrises in a big apartment downtown. I would match
with Chris on Hinge, and before our date, I would concoct
these elaborate fantasies about our future together, based on
one Instagram photo I'd seen of his family's lake house. All of
a sudden, I'd be thinking, "Yes, a June wedding at the Presidio
would be lovely. We'll have three kids and he'll be such a good
dad." Meanwhile, I've NEVER MET CHRIS. This is more than
a little disturbing.

I know plenty of friends who do this too. We get our hair
blown out for dudes who don't even own a passport. We get
our panties in a twist over someone who, for all we know, will
call the bartender "sweetie." And worst of all, we prematurely
decide a man is worthy of us. We've put him in the dating box

before we've seen any evidence (hence Reverse Box Theory, where unlike men, who put women in one of three boxes, we immediately put men in the dating box before they even deserve it). We've chosen them as our future husband, which, sorry to break it to you, is a weird first-date vibe. It makes you way more nervous than you normally would be, and it blinds you to who this person *actually* is and how the date is *actually* going.

It's like we are all microchipped with this falsehood that the entire goal of dating is to get guys to like us. And I get it, it's nice to be desired. But that is much more likely to happen if you don't act like you're going on a date with God's gift.

Get him off the pedestal. Collect your evidence. Here's how:

1. REMEMBER BOX THEORY: A dude probably isn't planning how to propose to you while you sip your vodka soda. He might be into you and want to date you, but until he shows you concrete proof, don't jump ahead and don't give him power over your feelings.

2. IMAGINE HIM TRIPPING on his shoelace, or unknowingly having food in his teeth. He's human, just like you. And he probably farted not long ago. Even Mr. Perfect says "You too" when the server tells him to enjoy his meal—fucking dork!

3. BE SCRUPULOUS: Evaluate him like you'd evaluate your best friend's new guy. A little harsher of a critic now, aren't we?

BOTTOM LINE: Don't future trip. Don't project an unearned image onto someone. Collect evidence based on what's in front of you.

THE SHIFT: This could be it! ⟶ We'll see!

Don't get me wrong, you can and should still be excited for the possibilities, and it's natural to get attached to the idea of someone more than the actual person. Just try to be aware of it and remind yourself to focus on how he makes you feel. It will lower the stakes, adjust your expectations, and allow you to have way more fun.

THE TALKING PHASE:

TEXTING MEANS EVERYTHING
AND IT ALSO DOESN'T MATTER

"If you're investing months of your time in someone,
make sure they want to hang out with you in real life."

—Tinx Original

Ugh, the talking phase. We've all been there, saying things like:

"I've been talking to this guy . . ."

"I matched with this guy and we've been talking ever since!"

"omg Jesse hit me up on Instagram and we've been talking like every day."

It seems harmless or even pretty exciting. I love a good text, which is essentially what the "talking phase" consists of. But there's a distinction I want to point out here: *"talking" ≠ hanging out ≠ relationship*. You can be pen pals with someone for months at a time, but if it never leaves the confines of your phones, it only creates a sense of false closeness. This seems to have become most prevalent among my younger besties who have always grown up with digital communication as the default. But the reality is that to really get to know someone, you need to be physically around them. You need to see which parking spot they choose or how they order a burrito. And above all—you need to get *out* of the talking phase, as it can keep you from ever establishing a real relationship. I've seen so many girls sink days, weeks, even months of their lives into a state of purgatory where they're essentially someone's Sudoku, something to do when the guy is mindlessly wasting time on his phone. You deserve better than that!

> **THE SHIFT:** Talking will lead to more, and we're on the way to a relationship! → Without in-person plans, we're on the road to nowhere

Now, I'm not a complete psycho who thinks that texting doesn't play a crucial role in the development of a relationship. Texting is what makes up the main part of the talking stage, *along with* a healthy dose of making plans and seeing how the guy treats baristas. It's also one of the most confusing things we have to deal with when it comes to dating in general. I'd say forty percent of the questions I get about dating involve when to text, what to text, what a text really means, or some other variation on deciphering messages from guys. And I get it. Texting can make or break a potential connection. There are layers. But we overcomplicate it. It's vital and reveals a lot and also doesn't matter. Got it?

Let me explain. If he likes you, you really don't need to worry about the content or frequency. He'll text you, the conversation will flow naturally, and you won't need to dissect every message and get your friends to proofread your every response. But let's be real—I wish it were ever that simple. The "to text or not to text" dilemma is one of the most universal human predicaments of our time. If you aren't sure where you stand, here are my core commandments:

Maintain the ratio. There are no rules about who should text first. You should feel empowered to text when you want. But you shouldn't be the only one reaching out. Initiating conversation should be equally balanced between the two of you. And please don't rationalize an imbalance by accepting the excuse "I'm terrible with my phone." *There's no such thing as a bad texter, only a lazy one.* Texting someone you're newly dating shouldn't be made to sound like it's some task that takes too much effort or that it's inconsequential enough to be forgotten—it's the most exciting and fun thing ever! If someone is constantly sending "sorry I'm the worst with texts" that's a cop-out.

Don't be question master. This is just a more specific subset of maintaining the ratio that goes beyond keeping the scales level and examines who is stoking the flames content-wise. When you're like "How was your day?" and they're like "Good" and then you're like "Nice! How was that thing you did at work?" and they respond with an answer but no continuation of the conversation . . . no further questions, Your Honor. Drop the inquisition until he gets a clue and asks you literally one thing. And if he doesn't? Let it die a peaceful death. This also applies to someone who texts frequently and makes conversation but doesn't make plans. Your time is valuable, and you can't get it back (something I wish I had internalized earlier in my life). *Change your behavior to see if it changes his. If it doesn't, move along.*

You never regret not responding. This might sound harsh, like a rule dreamt up by a scorned Virgo rising, but it really can apply to most situations. Especially if you're dealing with someone you're still unsure about. Basically, if you don't feel completely compelled to respond, if he *literally did not ask you a question*, you have no obligation to keep up the back-and-forth. In fact, it can actually benefit you to not. There's so much power in waiting half a day, turning your mind elsewhere, and then coming back to the conversation.

Note that I am not saying to wait an arbitrary amount of time to respond. If I see a text I will usually respond to it right away. I think it's a show of confidence. I'm secure enough to respond right when I see it instead of deliberating over it for hours. And it's such big-dick energy if a guy responds right away. I love it. When the texts are going back and forth rapid-fire, it's the closest thing to flirting in person, instead of both parties sitting there psychoanalyzing. So hot.

Clearly, I'm not a fan of a long lag (see "bad texter" bullshit above). But if you are doing mental algebra to figure out whether you should text, and it's really more of an itchy, burning compulsion to say SOMETHING, ANYTHING just to get another response back, then go do something else.

Of course, you may be thinking, "If I want to text him, I should be able to just text him." To which I say, abso-fucking-lutely. You can do whatever you want! My question is, where is it coming from? If it's just to scratch that itch and only for seeking validation, I wouldn't call that empowered texting. But if you have something to say, if you're out and see a billboard for the new James Bond movie and you two were just talking about your favorite Bond and you instinctively take your phone out to snap a photo and send it to him, by all means, don't overthink it. Send the fucking text. But if you are drafting a text to him in the Notes app on your phone, you are putting way too much weight on this. You have fallen prey to Reverse Box Theory and have him way too high up on the pedestal.

My whole point is, when the vibe is right, you shouldn't need to do that. You shouldn't need to read a forum on Quora to decide whether his text meant something more than what meets the eye. You shouldn't need a panel of judges on your group chat to crowdsource your next move. And you shouldn't need to spend a second of your time wondering if you should text him "Hey" with one or three *y*'s.

Instead of spending so much effort on texting, go and do something that makes you feel good. Work out. Meet up with a friend for coffee. Channel that energy into something that will give back to you.

I got this advice once from a friend and never forgot it: In the early stages of dating, communicate as if you're interested when you're with them, but you're not thinking about them when you're not with them. Be engaged, but don't act like you've been sitting around waiting for their texts. If they're in front of you, you're into it. If not, you're busy doing fun shit so they're not really top of mind.

Another thing I have to constantly remind myself because I get off on witty banter is that not every text has to be the most clever thing ever. Girls can spend so much time crafting a perfectly charming, flirtatiously sarcastic, breezy but bold text and it's not even appreciated for the Pulitzer-worthy work it is. It also brings that Reverse Box Theory energy to the text exchange—the guy can almost smell that you've put so much into the message. I look back on some of the texts I've sent and freaking cringe. I was quoting Chaucer in a text message once. So fucking embarrassing.

TLDR: It's not that deep. I'm not going to diminish the huge role of texting in modern dating, but these days it's too easy to get stuck in the talking phase. I mean, try asking your parents about it and watch them respond, "Wha?" Because the talking phase didn't exist until recently. People didn't have phones on them all the time, they had landlines and no call waiting and they had to make the effort to see whomever they wanted to actually talk to! Besides, I can almost guarantee that you are reading into each message wayyyyyy more than the dude on the other end. While you are trying to figure out what he meant by saying "ya" instead of "yea," he is watching some ESPN video about the most underrated quarterbacks of the eighties.

There's a concept in philosophy called Occam's razor, which essentially states that the simplest explanation is usually the best one. That's the case with men and texting. It works in multiple ways because not only does it mean that if they're not texting you, the simple answer is they aren't thinking about you, but also if they say "cool see you at 8," they genuinely mean cool, see you at eight. I'm not even saying this in a way that belittles men, like they aren't as deep thinkers. I actually think it's a strength that they say what they mean and don't overcomplicate things.

Honestly, we could all benefit from trying to text like a guy. Do your best to look at what's happening on the surface, not below it. Save the rest for an actual conversation.

"WHEN WE HANGING?"

AND OTHER THINGS THAT DON'T COUNT AS DATING

"I'm not a monkey, we are not hanging at all."

—Tinx Original

Nothing turns me off more than this phrase. It is the most lazy, passive, pick-the-lowest-hanging-fruit energy. The thing is, it's not even a real question. It's just a way for someone to reject all responsibility and ask the other person to do all the work.

"When we hanging?" is communicating the message that if you are put in front of me, I'm interested, but I don't care to make you a priority. I don't care enough about you to carve out time for you. But if you want to do all the work to make something happen, I might show up.

You deserve someone who actively wants to hang out with you and who will make it happen. Someone who can communicate clearly, make decisions, and plan ahead. The tough part is when you're in a scarcity mindset, you take any opening as a green light. A "When we hanging?" can sound like getting asked out on a date. But it isn't. It is the vocabulary equivalent of a seat filler. It's just . . . filling space.

I'm not saying they have to be like "I request her majesty Amelia Thermopolis Renaldi's presence for a FORMAL DATE." I'm just saying if a guy is using "When we hanging?"

I wouldn't classify it as anything more than a casual thing and a possible clue that you have been placed in the hookup box.

> **THE SHIFT:** "When we hanging?" →
> "Hey want to go to the movies this weekend? How's Sunday afternoon?"
> "A new Thai place just opened, do you want to try it with me?"
> "Was thinking we could grab dinner on Tuesday, are you free?"

You also want to keep an eye out for these "When we hanging?" dupes:

- "When am I seeing you?"
- "What's this weekend looking like?"
- "Supposed to be nice this weekend."
- "I'll be in your neighborhood on Tuesday."
- "What's your plan tonight?" (Ugh, I hate this one so much—might as well say "Are you going to be in the general vicinity of my dick tonight?")

Along those lines: just as "When we hanging?" does not equal "Let's go on a date," we need to clarify that there are certain situations that do not qualify as certified dates. These include:

- if you run into him and his friends on a Friday night and you end up bar hopping all night
- if you are both at a work event
- if you're both at a festival or concert or party and end up hanging together

Asking you on an actual date shows respect for you and, more important, offers a glimpse of how this dude will operate in a more serious relationship. Think about it this way: If you take on a "When we hanging?" guy, you will be signing yourself up for a long-term commitment consisting of "What's for breakfast?" "What did we get my parents for Christmas?" and "Can you make me a dentist appointment?"

I know this is hard because of another crippling condition that so many of us struggle with: Benefit of the Doubt Syndrome. You're always seeing the potential upside, thinking, "Well, you know, he put himself out there, I should meet him halfway," or "He's been really busy and stressed with work, I can't hold that against him," or "He had his brother in town this weekend and must have been showing him around." The thing is, you don't need to be making allowances. You are not his mother; you don't have to see the good no matter what. *Instead of seeing what could be, see what's in front of you.*

> **THE SHIFT:** Why would he ask "When we hanging?" if he didn't want to see me? ⟶ Why am I giving him the benefit of the doubt?

TINX'S CALENDAR CALCULUS:
YOUR CHEAT SHEET FOR DATING TIMELINE BEST PRACTICES

> "Rule No. 7, 'Never Accept a Date for a Saturday Night If He Asks After Wednesday.'"
>
> **—All the Rules (many of the rules in this book are trash IMO but I cosign this one)**

A word up top: In this section, I'm going to talk about ideal dating timelines. And yeah, I'm going to lay out a few rules. Remember that *Rules* book in the nineties? I mean, I didn't read it when I was five years old, but I've since become familiar with it. It told women exactly what to do to land a dude, when to sleep with him, and all the dos and don'ts to get you to the end goal: marriage. Obviously this is not that. But I do believe in the power of a system, a method to live by, and a way to take the guesswork out of "Should I or shouldn't I?"

This is partly why I invented Box Theory. It's a direct response to the "three-date rule" that urges women to wait until this arbitrary third date to have sex, like that's the magic number that hits some universal sweet spot in every man's mind/heart/dick. *The truth is, sex shouldn't be used as a manipulation tool, not because it's wrong but because it doesn't fucking work!* It doesn't change the way a guy feels about you, for better or worse. With Box Theory, you can liberate yourself from the idea that what you do or don't do will determine the way he feels about you, and instead focus on what you want to do. Fuck on the first date? Go off, Samantha Jones! Take it slow? We love an unhurried goddess!

> **THE SHIFT:** Sleep with him after X number of dates → Sleep with him whenever you want!

But let's back up. Timing comes into play long before you decide whether that Brazilian wax was worth it. For our purposes, I'm going to start the stopwatch the moment you match with someone on a dating app, since that's the most common way we land a first date these days. I'll walk you through exactly what a well-paced, sexy progression looks like and offer dos and don'ts that do NOT lead to marriage but save you time otherwise spent worrying and allow you to live your life (the real dream).

TINX'S PERFECT DATING TIMELINE:

After matching, you chat back and forth for twenty-four hours (I'm talking casual, quick convo—not exchanging your life stories).

He suggests and plans a date a couple of days in advance, including specific place and time. (Example: "Are you free for drinks Thursday? Okay great! Let's meet at Dan Tana's at 7.") The only time it's okay to agree to last-minute plans is if you're talking with the guy regularly, have already been on some dates, and he's like "Hey! I got off work early and am in your neighborhood—any chance you're free for dinner?!"

The difference is that he's thinking about you vs. a last-minute "wyd tonight?"

The day of the date—he should text that morning to confirm. If you don't have confirmation by 1:00 p.m., you don't go. This might sound like the most anal extreme rule I've ever made, but it's indicative of respect and viewing your time as important. I get messages from girls who are like, he hasn't confirmed and it's 6:00 p.m.! And I say, well, then you're not going, because regardless of whether you have other plans, it's totally disrespectful for him to think that you're just sitting around waiting for him. Even if it's not intentionally rude on his part, it's setting a precedent. And that's just not the vibe you want. If a dude follows up an hour before the date with a "we still on?" text, just send a savage yet classy message back along the lines of "didn't hear from you—made other plans!"

Okay, let's say everything has rolled out as it should and you're on the date. Some ground rules:

1. IT SHOULD BE DRINKS. (If you don't drink alcohol, it can be coffee or a walk, just avoid a movie or full-on dinner.)

2. IT SHOULD BE SHORT. Do not let it go longer than two drinks (a rule made by my genius friend Lindsey—hi, Lindz!). This is especially important when the date is going well. Good first dates are so exciting and the urge to keep it going is understandable. We've all been on those epic first dates that last like four hours, or even the whole day, or whoops now you're sleeping over and getting breakfast the next morning. I've done it, I've enjoyed it, and more power to you if you end up on a first-date bender. But we're talking ideal situations here, and thus, I have to say that long first dates tend to throw off the energy. It's hard to articulate exactly why, but let's just say it's best for both of you to be left wanting more. It allows for a more natural progression. As always, there are exceptions to this rule, but assume you're the rule, not the exception. Remember that the first date is just the metaphorical sniffing of each other's butts and asking, "Could there be something here?"

At the end of the date, you thank him IN PERSON as you're leaving. You do not text him that night, or the next day. You let him text you, because he will. (And if he doesn't, he doesn't like you. Hold a funeral, count it as a blessing that you have saved yourself precious time and energy, and move on to the next.) The important thing is not to trick yourself into thinking you need to reach out. You do not owe him a text or a thank-you— you thanked him at the end of the date, remember? You do not need to keep the conversation going for fear that he will forget about you. *If he likes you, HE WILL TEXT.*

The ideal time for him to text you after the date is the next morning. I love a 10:00 a.m. text along the lines of "Good morning, I had a great time last night. I would love to get sushi at that place I was telling you about soon." As a reward for having the self-control to not text him, you now get free reign to text him back as soon as you want to and with all the enthusiasm. Hit him back right away and don't play games in your response. Green light go!

The ideal timing for the second date is within a week of the first, if schedules allow. But don't move anything in your calendar to accommodate. In fact, it's good to show that you are busy. This is a great place to introduce one of my cardinal rules: NEVER CANCEL PLANS WITH GIRLFRIENDS FOR A GUY. (More on this in the Boyfriend Sickness chapter, which is a real doozy!)

From here, timing must be taken on a case-by-case basis, with two main overarching concepts to keep in mind:

1. FLIP THE CAMERA: Every time your focus is pointed outward (Does he like me? Is he thinking about me?), flip the camera back to selfie mode and ask yourself how you feel about him. Get specific and try to register your body's physical response to the thought of him—is it buzzy excitement? Or does it feel more like panic? Do you have to stifle an actual smile? Or do you grab your phone to check for the millionth time whether he's texted? Are you screenshotting every text conversation to send to your group chat or drafting every text in your Notes app before you send it? If so, he's not the one, honey. I actually think that in the early stages, it's more important to recognize how you feel when you're *not* with him vs. how you feel when you're with him. If you feel anything less than good and at peace, sit with that and remind yourself that the goal is not to get this person to like you but to find what makes you feel good.

> **THE SHIFT:** Is he gonna text? ➞ How do I feel when I'm not with him?

2. MATCH HIS ENERGY: Like I said above, it is not your responsibility to keep the momentum going. Let me tell you a little story to illustrate my point: There was a guy I started dating right when I moved to LA, let's call him Thad. He was an architect, and verrrrry sexy. We went out to dinner a couple of times and went on some hikes, but I was clearly in the hookup box. I just knew Thad was never going to seriously date me. But I was having the best sex of my life. His fuckboi tendencies were frustrating, but I just couldn't give up the D. I was in dicksand. I was dicknotized. So, I decided to match his energy. Not as a tactic to manipulate him into behaving differently, but as a better way for me to handle *myself* in the situation (and move on if needed). I made a conscious switch. I stopped texting him. I stopped caring so much. I started treating him like a booty call (just like he was treating me). I went on dates with other guys. And you know what? I got exactly what I wanted out of the relationship without sacrificing my self-worth.

> **THE SHIFT:** Should I text him? → Match his energy

Now, I am a very cut-and-dry person so these rules are easy for me to follow. But everyone is different, and I'm not saying that if the guy you're seeing doesn't follow these guidelines you have to cut him off completely. But I do think that staying on pace with him is important. Let's say you've gone on three amazing dates in two weeks, you're enjoying it and having fun, but he's kind of lost steam on texting you or making plans. Maybe don't save all your Fridays and Saturdays for him. Don't text him every day when he only responds half the time. *Bottom line: Don't lose your mind over someone who wouldn't mind losing you.*

FUCK ME SIDEWAYS:
SEX ON YOUR TERMS

"Graze on my lips, and if those hills be dry / Stray
lower, where the pleasant fountains lie."

–"Venus and Adonis," William Shakespeare

Sex is an incredible thing that a lot of women don't fully enjoy until way later than men do, for several very shitty reasons— the first being the incredible amount of shame we inherit and carry around in relation to our bodies. (It's no coincidence that this particular chapter has an unprecedented number of Shifts. The mental deprogramming we need to do when it comes to sex requires knocking down layer upon layer of social conditioning, so get your shift stick ready, ladies.) Another reason we tend to not get the satisfaction we want and need has to do with the misinformation about what sex should look and feel like. For example, the idea that a guy can just throw you up against a wall and go to town without so much as a drop of lubrication?! That is as unbelievable as any *Fifty Shades of Grey* nonsense.

Personally, these two hang-ups—being self-conscious about my body and being totally misled about what defines "good sex"—kept me from having good sex for most of my life. Honestly, they kept me from having sex at all until college. When I decided to rip the Band-Aid off (see how terrible our mindset around sex is?!) and lose my virginity to a water polo player at a cowabunga party (this might be perhaps the most California sentence ever written), I didn't tell him it was my first time. And afterward, he was like, "Damn, you're really good." I just smiled smugly while internally pumping my fist in the air because: goal of sex = he liked it, right?! I was so proud because I was "good at sex"—as if it were an act in a talent show and the judges had given me tens across the board. Never did I stop to ask myself, "How was it for me?"

For the rest of my college sexual experiences, I perfected my performance, focusing on sounding and looking a specific way because I thought it turned guys on. I said I liked whatever positions I thought guys liked. I would scream and moan as if I were auditioning for an adult film. Even when I got a serious boyfriend, I still treated sex as something to act my way through. I'm embarrassed to say this now but at the time, I would take pride in the fact that everyone in my sorority house would be like, "omg Tinx and her boyfriend have the loudest sex." In my mind, that was saying that I was great in bed. But the reality is that I didn't have an orgasm until after I graduated. And I was with my college boyfriend for three years! It wasn't his fault, though—that was on me. He would've done anything I asked, but I never asked for anything because I *didn't even know what to ask for in the first place*. My brain was so warped into thinking that I was strictly there to fulfill a guy's fantasy that I never explored my own desires. I didn't realize that sex could actually be based on what I was into.

> **I NEEDED A SHIFT:** What would he think is hot? → What gets me off?

Looking back, it is so insane that I basically thought sex was an acrobatics act. That it had to be tons of tricks and tools and stunts. Not only is that stuff usually not the surest path to pleasure, it puts the focus in the wrong place—all about what it looks and sounds like, not what it feels like. In most cases, no one else is watching you have sex (unless you have a webcam going, in which case go off, kink queen). For the rest of us, though, we need to shift our focus.

> **THE SHIFT:** What is it supposed to sound and look like? → What feels good to me?

The key to sex is getting out of your head and into your body. Keep the creepy porn director urging you to "arch your back" or "bite your lip" out of your mind. Instead of contorting yourself into a pretzel, just try to tap into the sensation. Relax your stomach—belly be damned. Let your eyes roll back in your head. Ignore the urge to play the role of hot sexy fantasy chick because in case I haven't made this clear: IT DOESN'T MATTER HOW YOU LOOK DURING SEX. A guy has never been mid-smash and called it off because he was so disgusted by a girl's butt pimple. In fact, I bet he never noticed it. It's like guys put on a pair of fogged-up glasses as soon as they hit the sheets—you can safely assume that you basically have a filter on that makes you look flawless. Your booty is in the eye of the beholder and the only thing he's worried about is whether he'll cum too fast. The more you lose yourself in the moment and stop freaking out about that stray nipple hair, the more he sees you actually ENJOYING WHAT'S HAPPENING, and thus, the hotter you will look. In other words: The time you spend figuring out how to sit on his face without him seeing your cellulite is time that you are stealing away from your pleasure—and his.

> **THE SHIFT:** What do I *look* like right now? → What does it *feel* like right now?

I remember the switch that happened in my sex life when I stopped the performance and just tried to figure out how I was wired and what got my jollies off. In my midtwenties, I finally started asking for what I wanted and asking my partners what they wanted and what felt good. The results were, dare I say, a sexual revolution. Let's compare and contrast:

HOW I HAD SEX IN MY TWENTIES:

- frantic, wild hookups with zero lead-up to doing the deed (rip each other's clothes off! That's passion, baby!)

- *loud* moaning; put on a show!

- whatever position I think he'll like, no matter how uncomfortable or exhausting

HOW I HAVE SEX IN MY THIRTIES:

- marathon-length, intellectual foreplay—we're talking flirty texts that lead into dinner that lead into a long make-out on the couch

- literally TALKING during sex!—forget what they told you in your writing workshop: tell, don't show

- figuring out what positions work for me (see: The Finisher)*

- following directions from *Cosmo* on how to "blow his mind in the bedroom"

- giving gentle directions to enhance my experience

- dirty talk taken straight from porn

- applying things I know my partner likes because we've had conversations about sex outside the actual bedroom

- worrying how I look afterward

- relaxing and laughing together in bed after (but please go pee first because UTIs are not it, honey)

---

* I've referenced this move before but never broken it down. I figure this tip right here is worth half the cost of the book. But anytime I've had to describe it I've literally had to climb onto a table or couch to re-create it, so we'll see how these instructions translate on the page. Basically, with the guy behind you, you lie on your stomach (a pillow underneath you is a nice touch). Then you tilt your hips at a diagonal so that one hip is pressing down into the bed with your leg straight and your opposite knee is hiked way up. Picture your lower half as a sexy number four. There are several reasons why this position is the best: 1. You're kind of contorted but actually super comfortable. You really don't have to do anything besides look insanely hot. 2. It creates all the right friction—he can go really deep but without stabbing your cervix and making you see stars. 3. Seriously, your body looks amazing at this angle. It is astonishingly flattering. 4. You can turn around and stare into his eyes. It's way sexier than a flat starfish and way more intimate than doggy style. 5. It lives up to its name. I dare a guy to last more than thirty seconds with this position.

Sometimes it takes someone special in your life to unlock this sexually empowered side of you. For me it was a guy I dated in my late twenties. We'll call him Brad. He was a total fuckboi. But I literally have never had better sex in my life, so we thank the king for his service and wish him nothing but the best. The reason the sex was so good was because he was just so open. We talked so much about sex. When I tell you we got SPECIFIC—exactly what we liked and all the things we thought made us weird in bed, which we came to find out are not weird at all and everyone's a bit of a freak so we just leaned into it.* Brad and I didn't just talk but really *listened* to what the other person was into, and then did it. I mean, it's not that complicated but boy was it the hottest thing ever.

Reader, you may be asking the question "What if you don't actually even *know* what feels good to you?" Worry not! The solution is quite literally in your hands (or handheld shower head or pillow or vibrator). The truth is that it's often much easier for women to get themselves off than to do so with a partner. So all you need to do is find what kind of wank works for you, and then translate it into sex with a partner. Get your body in a similar position, have them touch you in a similar way, or show them how to use the damn toy while you lie back and enjoy! Whatever you do, for the love of clitoris please don't hope that Chris is a mind reader. Your research must not be in vain. Communication is key.

---

* A little something juicy for my OnlyFans: Sometimes I like to film sex. Only with actual boyfriends. I love watching it afterward and sending it to them randomly in the middle of the day. Is there always the risk that it gets leaked publicly one day? Of course. But it worked out for Kim K., right?

A note here: You may have figured out your likes and dislikes, your kinks and your icks. But it's important to remind yourself (and clue in dear, sweet Chris) that what you like on one day might not be what you want the next (also, you can change your mind and preferences at any time). See, guys can be so eager to please that they take any morsel of insight a woman tells them about what she wants and consider it a blanket statement that applies to every single hookup. "She likes this," he tells himself, as he proceeds to replicate that thing he did with his tongue one time that got a good response. Imagine that your new boyfriend made you a spectacular pasta carbonara one night, and you raved about it. And then he made it for you the next night. And the next. Ad nauseam.

There are different types of sex for different moments. Sometimes you want wild, crazy, slightly rough sex (what a past boyfriend and I called "Saturday night sex"). And sometimes you've had a long week and just want some good old-fashioned, five-minute missionary. Imagine if you had shorthand and could just order the type of smangalang you're in the mood for?! The more you can get on the same wavelength, whether with fun code names you've established ("easy like Sunday morning, babe") or directly ("rail me, Daddy"), the sooner you can enjoy more satisfying sex. As my crisp-collared, rich-mom cookbook queen Ina Garten* would say, "How easy is that?!"

---

* I feel like she and her husband, Jeffrey, have a gorgeously healthy sex life. I read somewhere that for most of their marriage, they've spent weekdays apart and only see each other on the weekends, which has become my new relationship ideal.

However, I know many women still really struggle to use their voice in this way. I get asked all the time, "How can I say what I want in the bedroom?" and I know from experience that "easier said than done" is not always the case. I used to think it was so mortifying and corny to say things like "What turns you on?" But I've come a long way, thanks in large part to the aforementioned fuckboi and a few serious boyfriends who gave me the comfort level to suggest trying new things, to say what I wanted (no more pound town—slow sex is the number one secret to better sex in your thirties) and what I didn't like (for the record: doggy style—no thanks). Now I'm on the other end of the spectrum and I love asking the person I'm sleeping with really probing questions (once we're comfortable, of course) and making it feel really safe for them to tell me their preferences and fantasies.

I know how difficult it can feel to advocate for yourself in the most intimate way possible, but don't overcomplicate it. All you have to do is say, "Hey, I want to try this." Or "That doesn't really feel good to me, but I'd love if you'd . . ." I promise you that guys will think it's the hottest thing in the world and will be more than happy to follow directions. They literally aim to please.

Maybe you're at a loss and want me to just put words in your mouth? Fine. One of the hottest things you can say is just "Will you go down on me?" Nothing more, nothing less. Just drop that on him and see him pitch a tent quicker than a Boy Scout. So many girls write to me feeling so embarrassed to assert themselves in this way. But here's the thing: *The more confident you are, the more attractive you'll be. The more you advocate for yourself, the more it will turn a guy on, because it means that you've taken the time to know your body and value yourself enough to ask for what gets you off.*

That said, I get that if you haven't done this before, it can be nerve-racking to initiate this conversation, so let me get the ball rolling for you. Here is an Onboarding Survey you can administer to any potential partner. As they say, the more you know, right?!

Name: _____

STI tested? _____

Agreed-upon form of protection/birth control: _____

What are your turn-ons? _____

_____

Where is your favorite place to be touched/teased? _____

_____

What is your favorite type of foreplay? _____

_____

Favorite sex position? _____

_____

What's the hottest thing to say or hear during sex? _____

_____

Morning sex or late-night sex? _____

Sexting—hot or awk? _____

What is something you've always wanted to try? _____

_____

Any secret fantasies? _____

_____

Any no-go situations for you? _____

_____

On a scale of 1 to 10, how hot do you find me and
what specific things make me a 10? _____

_____

I know I'm talking a big game about good sex, but let's have a word about bad sex, because there is a time and place for it: the first hookup with someone new. Let's face it, contrary to what Kate Winslet's hand in the steamy car scene from *Titanic* would tell you, the first time you do the deed with someone is often more clunky than climactic—whether you're in a car or not. And how could it not be? You're not even comfortable eating a sushi hand roll in front of him, how could it feel easy-breezy to figure out how his crooked dick fits best inside you?

I find it helpful to apply the Open House Analogy to first-time hookups. Think of them like a house tour—you're exploring a new space, seeing if you like the vibe. You're probably going to have follow-up questions. You're probably going to need to make a few modifications—a coat of paint here, a different light fixture there. But you can't spend too much time at the open house—you're just scouting the location to see if you can see yourself spending more time there in the future. Don't get hung up on the way it's staged or things that can easily be changed to your liking. Ask yourself: Does this house have good bones? Does this dude's plumbing work? Is our foundation solid? Do we have structural integrity? For the right house, we can take on a fixer-upper.

> **THE SHIFT**: Was the sex too bad to give it another shot? → Do I like him enough to give it another shot?

Let's briefly address sending nudes as well, since it's not something they cover in sex ed. I'm often asked, "When is too early to send a nude?" and I say the perfect time is whenever you're comfortable with it—unless you're underage, in which case there are legal ramifications (and you're probably on your parents' phone plan so let's just not). I personally love sending nudes, but they are more for me than the guy. They turn me on, just feeling sexy and knowing that they will elicit such an, um, excited response. But obviously you have to have some trust built into the relationship. Unfortunately the threat of revenge porn is all too real and you don't want your photos being used against you in the future. Just assume that anything you send could always end up being seen by more than just the recipient, so you have to be aware and okay with the risk. (When I first started working with my manager Sethy he asked if there were any nudes out in the universe and I was like oh lord you better sit down.)

I guess if I had to sum up the message here, it would come down to one simple philosophy: Overcommunicate, but don't overcomplicate. At the end of the day sex is two people in a room (okay, sometimes more people, sometimes you're outside) and the hottest thing is someone taking the time to get to know your body and what turns you on. Don't stand in the way of that.

A HOT GIRL'S GUIDE:

HOW TO TRAP A FUCKBOI

"This bloke's come in here and sucked me into his dicksand."

—Olivia Attwood, *Love Island*, Season Three

Ah, the elusive fuckboi. An extraordinary species who mates with many, many females while having no intentions of establishing a relationship. He can camouflage himself effectively enough to disguise his extremely douchey nature, and he has lured many an intelligent victim into mating by offering the seductive promise that she is the one and only woman able to trap and tame him.

I've been in the Wild West a long time. I can smell a fuckboi from a mile away. I can see his tracks in the sand. I know when he's within a twenty-mile radius. I could tell you how to trap one, skin one, wear one as a coat. As far as fuckboi trapping goes, I'm Crocodile Dundee. I've wrangled some real beasts in my time. Some that I can't even talk about here. (Because they're famous!) Could I tell you how to set a booby trap that no fuckboi could escape? Sure, but I'm not going to and here's why: It is a completely fruitless expedition.

Because once you trap a fuckboi, you have to take the beast home. And then you've got a wild animal in your house. And while you might feel a momentary flash of pride, let me tell you, it will be short-lived. Because how you get them is how you lose them. Never forget that. If you have to wrangle and trick and manipulate a fuckboi into your home, that's exactly how he'll leave, sneaking out the back door and leaving you bamboozled.

Have some fuckbois settled down and become loving husbands? Of course. Can people change? Absolutely. Should you be the one to change them, or wait around until they do? Nope. Killer whales can be kept in captivity, but the trainer often ends up without an arm or dead at the bottom of the tank. You are not a fuckboi trainer. Nor are you a rehab center for someone who needs maturity and therapy. *The second you go on a crusade to change someone, you are elevating their importance in your life higher than your own.* You're saying that rather than calling someone of equal worth into my life, I'm going to try to rehabilitate this dude. If you were reading about this in a book or watching it on TV, you'd be like, "Why is she doing this?" But we do it all the time. Why? Because of ego.

Nobody loves a fuckboi more than a big ol' ego that whispers in your ear, *You could be the one to change him.* It convinces you that you and only you hold the power to convert the fuckboi into some perfect loyal boyfriend. Our ego is the one who fancies herself Indiana Jones and says, "Get your hat on, we're going to catch us a fuckboi." But you need to ask yourself, to what end? The whole idea of a bad boy changing for the right girl is something made up for movies. Smart girlies who know better say, "I wouldn't touch that with a ten-foot pole. I've got better things to do with my time."

This is not coming from a place of judgment. I spent two very painful years trying to wrangle a fuckboi and an entire summer trying to capture one of the most famous fuckbois in the world. Both times I ended up with my dick in my hand. I know now that a relationship based on denying who the person is in that very moment is doomed before it begins. I've hung up my hat. Fuckboi season is over.

> **THE SHIFT:** I can change him ⟶ Why would I want to?

DATA COLLECTION:

HOW TO WORK THROUGH THE TANTRUM AND KEEP THE SCENT GOING

"Let's do it. Let's go get the shit kicked out of us by love."

—Sam, *Love Actually*

When I was twenty-three, my roommate Molly and I lived in a beautiful purple house on Laguna Street in San Francisco that felt somewhere between living in a sorority house and being on *The Real World*. We were navigating those high highs and low lows of the first years out of college, where you have no idea what you're doing but you're working like crazy while trying to hold on to the lifestyle you had in college, but also now you have bills to pay and can't get loaded fries at the dining hall at two o'clock every Sunday afternoon so it's just kind of exhausting.

We had this thing called The Tantrum, where you come home from work at like seven thirty and you have thirty minutes to get ready to go on a date. So you spiral. You think, "Why the fuck am I going to waste fifteen dollars of makeup and put on a whole new outfit to go meet some dude named Bryant and have him tell me about his startup over a shitty vodka soda?" Molly and I would alternate going through it, wanting to cry and cancel and crawl into bed all at once. But we would encourage whoever was having The Tantrum to go because here's the thing: **Dating is a numbers game, and you have to play to win.**

There's also this thing called The Scent* that you get when you go on a date, even if you're not that excited about it. It's a magical feeling that can only be produced when you put yourself out there. When you keep The Scent on you it gives off an air of desirability and sexy energy. It changes the way you feel and even when the actual date is a big stinker, your aroma stays stronger for the next one.

Back in the purple house days when we felt like we just couldn't be bothered to go on another shitty date, Molly and I would each fill an enormous cup with ice and drink this awful white wine called Santa Margherita through a straw (while blasting that Drake song where he says "Santa Margherita by the liter . . .") and just sit on the landing, half screaming, half crying that we simply could NOT go, which would somehow gear us up to go on that Hinge date at Blue Light with another Chris wearing a Chubbies button-down. This much I know is true: You have to allow The Tantrum, and you need a girlfriend to get you through it.

So the next time you are having a predate spiral, put on a song that gets you going. Have maybe a half glass of wine or a little tequila on the rocks. Grab your roommate or call your best friend and tell her you're having The Tantrum. Label your emotions and embrace them. Then look at yourself in the mir-

---

* Concept inspired by *Sex and the City*, which I guess also applies to just about everything in this book.

ror and say, "This is what life is. You're a taxpayer now and this is the tax you pay for dating. You're going to go for an hour and even if it's a terrible time it'll be a good story." Know that if the date doesn't result in anything more than small talk and a mild hangover at work the next day, you're doing it right. You have to go on bad dates, boring dates, dates that feel like a waste of time. You gotta get those reps in.

> **THE SHIFT:** What's the point of going on all these useless dates? → It's all data collection, baby

When you make that shift in thinking about dating as a numbers game, it is actually way less fatiguing because you're not putting as much pressure on each date, and if it doesn't work out, you chalk it up as another successful session instead of a waste of time. Rather than seeing each first date as "starting over," you see it as building upon your data sample. You're not focused on the outcome but the scientific process.

Of course, there are things you can do to make the whole thing easier on yourself. Always try to schedule the date close to your house. No back-to-back dates—you need a rest day in between. And feel free to set a one-hour or two-drink boundary and then scurry back home. It's okay to feel fatigue, but don't talk yourself out of a date because, the truth is, most aren't bad. Maybe some are boring, but most are at least a little fun once you're actually there.

This also brings up the entire definition of a "good" vs. "bad" date. Our thinking is so narrow-minded in this regard. When we get home from a date and our roommate asks how it went, it's always, "Did you kiss at the end of the night? Do you think you'll see him again?" Never do we ask, "Did you learn something about yourself?" It doesn't even have to be something profound—it could be that you found a new bar you love. Or a fun fact you didn't know before.

I will always remember a horrific date I went on not because it was god-awful (it was) but because he took me to this cool underground sake place, and now that's my go-to date spot in New York. I consider it a great date because it showed me something I never would have known existed otherwise.

There was another time I hung out with this hipster guy named Woods Buckley (which is just the perfect hipster name), who invited me over to his house to make pie (which is just the perfect hipster date). I made a cherry pie, he made a peach one. We got drunk and had the best time. He played this song called "Off & On" by Dickystixxx, and it became my favorite song. Like, literally my top song on Spotify in 2017. Unfortunately he just wanted to be friends even though I would've married him on the spot. But I'm so grateful for that drunken pie-making date because it gave me something that has brought me so much joy. My point is, sometimes all you get is a song. Sometimes all you get is a new bar. *A good date is not one where you meet your next boyfriend.* Sometimes it's a date where you try Ethiopian food for the first time. And that's beautiful.

Besides, I barely remember those one-off, nightmare dates, but boy do I remember those tantrums that got me to put on my GOT (Going-Out Top) and brave another Thursday night at Blue Light, and then have the customary postgame recap session with my girlfriends after the date. I look back on those times in that purple house, getting ready with friends, dancing around, and helping each other pick out which frilly top and 7 for All Mankind jeans to wear, as some of the happiest times in my life.

> **THE SHIFT:** I cannot go on one more date ➔ I might not end up dating this guy, but I sure as hell will remember and miss these moments with my girlfriends

ICK LIST:

THE ANTI-CRUSH LIST

Joel: "I can't see anything that I don't like about you."

Clementine: "But you will!"

—Eternal Sunshine of the Spotless Mind

If the crush list is about hope and possibility, the ick list* is about bursting that bubble. You know when you're dating someone and you're in the stage where everything they do is perfect? And then one day you see that their toothbrush looks like it hasn't been replaced in years? You let it slide, but it makes you a little less horny for them. Well, instead of sweeping it under the rug, recording it for future reference can be very useful. An ick list is essentially a pros and cons list but without any pros, and all the cons are relatively minor offenses that you let go because you ultimately like the guy.

What is the purpose of an ick list? It helps combat Reverse Box Theory for people like me who are prone to future tripping. I'll meet an interesting guy and before he's even finished

---

* I've taken the term "ick," popularized by *Love Island* contestant Olivia Attwood and memeified by TikTok, and adapted into a list-based tool, because I am a millennial woman.

the first sentence I'm like "omg he's so eloquent" and then I go and take the paint-by-numbers kit and fill in the rest myself, painting a picture that's more aspirational than realistic. If I'm in a relationship, it's even worse—I'm obsessed with the way he holds the steering wheel and get weak in the knees just looking at the back of his neck. I experience emotions very deeply, to the point where it feels like I'm on drugs. So I've found the ick list to be a helpful tool to calm me down and bring me back to earth. It's an antidote to the crush list, where instead of putting love goggles on, we take them off and make someone human.

Here's how it works. Just like with the crush list, you can start a simple note in your phone (and by all means, bury it deep within an inconspicuously titled list of "Things to Get at Bed Bath & Beyond"). And then anytime they do something weird or you notice something that gives you an ick (e.g., wow, he is thirty-four years old but doesn't have a headboard!), catalog it.

Your icks do not need to make sense to anyone but you. They are extremely personal and you do not need to defend or even explain them. One of my exes held his fork really weird, like a caveman. Was it a fatal flaw? No. But did it take him a little bit off the pedestal? You better believe it. I never mentioned anything to him about it because I didn't want to make it an issue or be a snob about it. Until he was a giant dick to me. Then I whipped out my ick list and remembered the Neanderthal grip, and it made our breakup a little easier.

Please note that this is for relatively minor grievances, not major red flags. If the guy you're dating is getting blackout drunk and picking fights with you, that's not ick-list material. But if he calls his mom "mommy"? Log it.

Look, in the rest of this book I am preaching some very self-actualized, evolved advice. But when it comes to the ick list? I urge you to be petty. Maybe he watches standup comedy and then tries to pass the jokes off as his own. Maybe he has terrible taste in shoes. If he's the guy for you, these things can be endearing or at least endurable. This is not about making fun of or picking apart men, it's about combating Reverse Box Theory and the tendency that women have to get wrapped up in the *idea* of the guy they're with while ignoring the wonderfully flawed, real person that he is. Ick lists can also be incredibly helpful when you need to evaluate the relationship. If you feel yourself getting too attached too quickly, you can review the ick list and remind yourself that he is a normal and imperfect person like the rest of us. Or if he ghosts you or it doesn't work out, you can refer back to it and think, PHEW.

THE SHIFT: He's flawless! ⟶ He farts in his sleep

POV:
MAIN CHARACTER ENERGY

"I live for the nights that I can't remember /
With the people that I won't forget."

—Drake, "Show Me a Good Time"

Main character energy is a trend that originated on TikTok. And it ties directly into The Shift because it's all about reframing your mindset, putting yourself first, and living your life in a way that focuses on your journey and places your wants and needs at the center of the story. Put simply, you make yourself the main character in the movie of your life and live life accordingly. And we love that for us!

Shifting your perspective to main character energy is extremely clarifying when you ask yourself what your next move should be in an early relationship. For example, would the main character sit around staring at their phone waiting on Chris to call them? Or would they put on some Kacey Musgraves, pour themselves a whiskey, and go out to find their next meet-cute? Would the main character fall into a black hole on Instagram looking at all of Chris's followers for clues about his life? Or would the main character go on a girls' trip to Palm Springs where they end up singing Frank Sinatra on a baby grand piano at two in the morning?

This doesn't mean that you have to live your life like every night is New Year's Eve and you've made a bet that involves finding your soulmate at the stroke of midnight in Grand Central Terminal. Main characters can definitely spend a quiet night in, reading a new book and drinking exactly one and a half glasses of wine. But what main characters *aren't* doing is spending the entire evening ready to ditch their solo night the moment Chris suggests last-minute plans. The plans that main characters make with themselves are just as important as the plans they make with others.

Imagine your life as a Netflix movie. You are not playing the quirky friend; you do not have a quick cameo. The POV is YOU. When you are embodying main character energy, you can look at your crush list like you are a casting director deciding who is going to appear on-screen. You can scout a location to see if it will work for you. You can try on everything in your closet during a fun little montage sequence.

Main character energy is a lifestyle. It is a way of being in the world that encompasses the important stuff and the tiny details. In case you need me to break it down further, main character energy includes:

- being busy and excited about what's on your calendar
- using "No" as a complete sentence
- celebrating your friends' wins
- taking risks, like asking a guy out
- going on a walk by yourself while listening to an audiobook
- staring out the plane window during takeoff while listening to a hyperspecific playlist

- ordering fries for the table
- not being afraid to cry
- not being afraid to ask questions, speak up in meetings, or say "I don't know"
- not being afraid to fail (see it as a plot twist!)
- knowing what you love but still being curious about what you don't understand
- letting the adventure of the day unfold, which might mean that yes, you went on a hike and ended up taking shots of tequila in your workout clothes but that's the way this episode rolled out

And in case you need more clarity on what is NOT main character energy: Your friends say on Tuesday, "Hey, we're going to go to a winery on Saturday! Do you want to come?" and you've been seeing this guy and you think he *might* ask you to hang this weekend and you just have this inkling because he kind of mentioned it halfway and so you say no to your friends because you're gonna wait to see if this guy will ask you. In the name of everything holy—do not do this! Even if you say yes to your friends and the guy ends up asking you out, do not cancel on your friends. Not only is it minor character energy, it is actually more attractive for a guy to know that you are active and social and that if they snooze on asking you out, they lose.

Main character energy can also help put a positive spin on things when there's change afoot. For example, moving to a new city can be incredibly stressful and lonely, but when you think about it as the main character making a big move, it's exciting. Who will she meet? What surprises are in store?

Similarly, when bad things happen, this can be a comforting

lens to see things through. Instead of freaking out about your ex's new girlfriend suddenly becoming your cubicle mate, you can just insert voice-over commentary that observes, "Now things are getting interesting." Or when Chris ends up being a total dud, you can shrug your shoulders and conclude, "Guess he wasn't the leading man."

When you embody main character energy, you can have courage and confidence knowing that whatever comes your way, that's just the arc of your narrative. This is all just following the script.

> **THE SHIFT:** Why is this happening to me? ➝ Oooooo, the plot thickens!

RMW:

THE NONNEGOTIABLES OF YOUR LIFE

"IT'S A VIBE"

—Workout tank

One of the pillars of my core belief system—in addition to Box Theory and using spoons to more efficiently inhale my salads (shout-out to my Shovel Gang)—centers around being a Rich Mom.

It all started as a fun joke, taking photos of my outfits and inventing Rich Mom personas to go with each one (for example, "Hamptons Mom tries to be 'chill' as she watches in horror while her nanny allows toddler Frederic to eat complex carbohydrates for breakfast") and creating "Rich Mom starter pack" videos with hyperspecific regional markers of Rich Mom culture (from the Rich Mom Aspen Edition: "Only be seen at the Caribou Club, a safe haven where you can black out in private"). But from there, it took on a life of its own, symbolizing a larger message of wanting the best for yourself.

Now, while I aspire to become a *literal* RICH MOM one day, let me be clear that you do not need to be rich and/or a mom to embody this lifestyle. It's not a specific status symbol, it's an energy. It's about taking good care of yourself so you can show up for the other people who need you. It's about buying yourself a fancy coffee because you deserve it and cooking yourself a steak at 9:00 p.m. because you feel like it. More specifically, for me it has become a nonnegotiable to go on a Rich Mom Walk (RMW) every day, no matter what is going on in my life.

If being a Rich Mom is my religion, going on a RMW is my daily devotional practice. Rich Moms are extremely busy, with a lot of demands pulling at us from all sides. We are the most at risk of catering to everyone else's demands while sacrificing our own. So the RMW is an act of resistance. Our church is the open road/treadmill, and the sermon of the day could be a favorite podcast (*cough cough* *It's Me, Tinx*?!) or our beloved therapist. The important thing is that come what may, we put our yoga pants on, get those steps in, clear our heads, and get a fresh perspective.

I mention this here in a book about dating because it's an extension of main character energy and the overall message of shifting your perspective from external validation to internal maintenance and self-knowledge. An RMW is the thing that makes me feel centered, but different strokes for different folks. A walk around the block might not be your Rich Mom cup of tea, but it's important to figure out what is—and make it a nonnegotiable.

> **THE SHIFT:** I'm too busy! ⟶ I'm worth it

SOFTWARE UPDATE:

DATING IN OTHER CITIES

"The energy you put out comes back to you."

—Eckhart Tolle

I think one of the best things that you can do when you're young and single is go on dates in other cities. If you're on vacation or visiting friends who live far away, or even if you're on a business trip, set your dating app location to whatever city you're in and go on a date. Here's why: First of all, it's a much better way of seeing the city and getting a tour from a local. Second, it gets The Scent on you (see page 62). Third, it is the most carefree form of dating because you are already in a more adventurous mindset and you have way fewer expectations. Fourth, you are the best version of yourself on these dates, because even if you are not the kind of person who does interview questions on a first date, even if you are in no way dating to get married, you typically have *some* goal or intention on a date in the city you live in. There is a freedom that comes with going on a date where the only goal is to meet a cool person and explore a new city.

When I was living in New York, my friend set me up with this guy who lived in LA while I was out there on a trip. We went out on the last night I was there and had such a good

---

time. We had drinks at Shutters in Santa Monica and a truly transcendent dinner at Elephante. He was a bit older, and we didn't have much in common, but we enjoyed each other's company. We did end up having a flirty long-distance back-and-forth for a couple of months, and I probably should have ended things much sooner than I did because ultimately he just wasn't that fun to be around and he made me feel insecure. But looking back, I think I was the best version of Tinx on that first date because I had zero expectations and just had fun.

Then in November 2020, I found myself living in LA and going through tons of big changes. I had just broken up with New Guy (more on him later), was still madly in love with Friend (we'll get to him as well), and I had to go to New York for work. I did not have the mental capacity for a relationship, but I decided to go on a date with this sexy restaurateur. Let's call him . . . Sexy Restaurateur. He was *so* New York—such a nice contrast to all my LA guy friends and dating prospects. He wore a suit and was just so suave and worldly. I never even slept with him, but we went on a lot of fun dates, he took me to all these incredible restaurants, we would walk his cute dog all over the city, and he really helped me remember that there was a side of me that loved the culture I wasn't getting in LA. I'm definitely a sponge that takes on the style and energy and interests of whomever and whatever I'm around, and LA had immersed me in the "content creator" world while making me forget the cosmopolitan side of myself that loved theater and art and books that weren't self-help. Sexy Restaurateur brought that side of me back into the light and made me feel smart and powerful, all in front of the backdrop of a city I loved but didn't have any roots in. He wasn't ultimately my guy, but he really liked me and I really liked him, and he got The Scent back on me so that when I went back to LA I felt rejuvenated and hopeful.

THE SHIFT: Dating should lead you to your soulmate →
Dating should show or remind you of different sides of yourself

Look, we all get in ruts sometimes. Lord knows I love a routine, but it can get stale. Dating in other cities is a great way to shake up your everyday, refresh your vision of yourself, and remember parts of your personality you may have forgotten. It's like a reset—all you need to do is unplug yourself from the power source and plug yourself back in.

Let's say you're visiting Chicago. You go on a date with a great guy. He is low-key obsessed with you, you guys are flirting like mad, it makes you feel so incredible. You're relaxed, you feel hot and desirable and fun. You're the best version of yourself. You have The Scent all over you. Then you get back to your city and you're like, ugh, there are no good guys here.

That's a complete lie. Let me tell you the truth. *There is a soulmate for you. In every single city.* There's probably a couple, okay? But you have to remember to be that person you were on your trip if you want to attract the same kind of vibes. Have a little snog with someone in Chicago, and then bring that attitude back home with you! Don't forget who you were while you were traveling. *Give off the energy that you want to receive.* Remind yourself, "I'm not the girl who asks how many kids he wants on the first date. I'm actually super fun. And I love going to dive bars and drinking beer and talking about *Star Wars.*" I would go so far as to say that if you're feeling in a rut, schedule a little getaway if you can. Check out a new city, get The Scent on you, and then channel that person on your own turf.

THE SHIFT: There are no guys in my city ⟶ I'm going to explore other cities to discover different sides of myself

BEWARE, HAZARDS AHEAD:

GHOSTING, BREADCRUMBING, AND LOVE BOMBING

"You can't win if I'm not playing."

—Tinx Original

In this chapter, we will be covering three of the worst offenses you can be hit with while dating. Let's start out with the one we are all probably most familiar with.

GHOSTING

You went on a date with Chris, you had a great time, maybe you hooked up, maybe you didn't, but without any explanation you never hear from him again. Leaving you to wander the hallways of your mind like a feral banshee, pulling your hair out and wailing, "Why?!"

I'm not going to sit here and tell you that you shouldn't let it affect you. If you can see a ghost and come away from it like "whatever," then hats off to you, girlfriend, but for the rest of us, we are spooked and need to work through it.

First and foremost, we need to understand why ghosting happens. This requires a shift right up top.

THE SHIFT: What did I do? ⟶ It's not about me

I know it's hard not to take ghosting personally, but I promise you, if a guy ghosts it is one hundred percent about him not having the confidence to express himself. Because let's face it—it's not that hard to send a text saying, "Hey, it was nice getting to know you, but I'm just not feeling the vibe." The fact that he cannot do that says all you need to know about how he handles anything that presents more difficulty than remembering his Hulu password. The petty side of me would call it small-dick energy. The more evolved version of me would urge you to think about what it would be like to go through life with someone who can't even send a simple text. Do you really want to drag a useless, soggy mop around with you? Girl, he did you a favor. You'll look back on this and think, thank goodness that didn't work out. It made space for something miraculous.

> **THE SHIFT:** Rejection hurts → Rejection is redirection

This ties back to Reverse Box Theory—when a guy drops off the map unexpectedly, it can give you amnesia and make you forget whether you were even that into him in the first place. It's clear you're hurting, but it's easy to misdiagnose it as sadness over losing someone, when in fact it's not your heart that's bruised, it's your ego. Your ego is what felt like this guy was a conquest that it lost. Your ego was just out to get validation and now it feels rejection, which is a tough pill to swallow. Try to be honest with yourself about the connection (or, more realistically, lack thereof) instead of letting your brain attach unearned meaning to this person. Did you *really* want him or are you just pissed he had the audacity to dismiss you?

Regardless, your anger is justified, but if you're thinking

about sending him a text to give him a piece of your mind, let me slap the phone out of your hands right now. Of course you want to call this fucker out. But let's play this all the way through—what are you going to get out of it? A text that says, "yea sorry I didn't like you enough"? You don't need confirmation. Actions speak louder than words. Don't waste another second of your time. Flip to the next chapter to learn how to hold a funeral so that you can move on. Something better is coming.

BREADCRUMBING

If you easily fall victim to Reverse Box Theory, you also have a much greater chance of being breadcrumbed. This is when a guy doesn't fully ghost you but he will leave you little totems of hope. Let's say you go on a date with Chris. It was like a four out of ten, but you had hyped him up so much in your mind that you went into the date totally blinded by your expectations. You don't even really remember what the two of you talked about because you were just so desperate to get Chris to like you.

You didn't really have anything in common with him, but you convinced yourself there was a connection, because . . . he said he liked tacos too and that's kinda serendipitous, right?! After not hearing from Chris the day after the date, you go on Instagram and see that he is one of the first people to view the story you just posted. Holy shit. This is a sign from Chris and his repressed emotional skills that he actually does want to date you. Despite the fact that he hasn't texted you. Despite the fact that you have zero shared interests beyond tacos. This is definitely a sign.

So what do you do? You decide with the help of an entourage of your friends to text Chris, "Hey, thanks for drinks last night. I had the best time!" Eight hours later, Chris responds, "Yeah, me too. It was fun. We should do it again sometime." WE SHOULD DO IT AGAIN SOMETIME?! You screenshot it and send it to the group chat. This is proof that he's actually obsessed with you.

A few days go by. Chris has not set that second date. So what do you do? You pray. You manifest. You sleep with his name under your pillow. A few more days go by. You post a rather sexy story on your Instagram that Saturday night, feeling particularly bold after two Aperol spritzes. An hour later, Chris responds to your story with "looking hot." Well, fuck me sideways, HE'S BACK.

Wrong. Chris has also had a couple of drinks that Saturday and is sitting there bored on the couch waiting for his turn to play *Call of Duty*. He shot off a response with the same amount of effort it takes to scratch his balls. But you take it as a symbol of his interest. This is a love story for the ages.

The next week, you are still convinced that you and Chris are meant to be. You see that Tame Impala is coming to play in your town. You remember (you think?) that you and Chris talked about your mutual love of Tame Impala—yet another point of connection, your souls are entwined! So what do you do? You text Chris, "omg Tame Impala is playing here on Friday. It's gonna be so good." Chris responds, "ya it's gonna be epic. we should definitely go."

At this point, you are naming your future children. You have swept yourself into a complete frenzy and are beside yourself with the news that you're going to a show together like the #couplegoals you are. You text the group chat to tell your friends, and they respond, "That's amazing! When did he ask you? Did he already get tickets?" Hmmm. *Technically*, he didn't ask. Or get tickets. He simply did the bare minimum by responding to a text. But why would he respond if he wasn't interested? Maybe because he's trying to be nice. Maybe because he's bored. Maybe because he felt bad he hadn't texted you back before. Whatever the case, the fact remains: He did not ask you to go to Tame Impala.

By now you have wasted a month of your precious life on Chris, from the predate fantasies to the aforementioned nondate. Yes, he continues to keep the conversation going, but let's be real, he is literally just punting the ball back to you as you sprint back and forth, grunting that insane tennis grunt and flinging your racket around. (Me: Goes to the US Open once . . .)

Men do have a kind of radar that tells them just when you've started to move on, prompting them to poke their head back in the doorway and maintain their hold over you (see "Men Always Come Back or Their Lives Get Worse," page 141). But if you aren't even in an established relationship with them yet, it's far more likely that you're projecting way more significance onto the situation. Unless he is texting you saying, "Hey want to grab dinner on Thursday around 8?" don't take anything as a sign.

Ultimately, you need to ask yourself: Am I willing to settle for someone who feeds me breadcrumbs? Is that a diet I can maintain long-term? If not, take the blinders off and when you see crumbs, recognize them for what they are and throw them at the pigeons.

LOVE BOMBING

Lord almighty this is perhaps the biggest mindfuck in the entire book. Love bombing was originally coined as a term to describe the psychological manipulation used to influence and exploit someone, and it's been utilized by abusive parents, cult leaders, and romantic partners alike. As it applies to dating, it's like ghosting and breadcrumbing on steroids and is far more blindsiding because the other person has actually promised you the moon and the stars. So gather round, Bomb Squad, and I will show you how to identify a love bomber at work.

At their core, love bombers are narcissists who are driven by a deep need for admiration. In the first couple of weeks of the relationship, they will be extremely attentive and loving and use a lot of flowery language. They might talk a lot about the future and all the things they want to do with you. They might use "we" very early on. They might even say "I love you" pretty quickly and make you feel very safe.

They promise you the world, and then all of a sudden do a bait and switch, dropping you completely or heavily scaling back. It's a massive manipulation tool that leaves you confused and desperate to get back what you had. And if they're really cruel, they'll continue a spree of serial love bombing, pulling you back in, playing hot and cold, and making you addicted to chasing the feeling you lost.

Now, I'm not saying that you can't believe anything a guy says in the early days. But you need to ask yourself whether what he's saying is based on the actual foundation you two are standing on or if he's saying it to make you (and himself) feel good. If you haven't known someone for that long and he's saying he's going to take you to a B&B in Carmel for your three-week anniversary, what is that based on? Yes, sometimes there is an instant connection and whirlwind romance, but in that case, you can call my bullshit from the patio of the B&B he *actually* took you to and I will Venmo you mimosa funds.

I was casually dating a celebrity not long ago, which is a gross humblebrag I fully take responsibility for, but the point is that he told me he was going to build me a house in Santa Barbara. You better believe I pushed the alarm button and called in the bomb threat right away. I straight-up told him, "I know what you're doing! We haven't even spent a full day together yet!" The annoying thing about it was that it felt so good to hear it in the moment, but I knew exactly what was going on.

You can't help the sparks going off in your brain when you hear that a guy wants to marry you or introduce you to his mom. But I've learned the hard way to crave very different things in the early days of a relationship. I know it's not as exciting when a guy calls you and says, "Hey, do you want to go to the movies on Thursday?" But you know what? That's real.

As they say, a bird in the hand is worth two in the bush, and a guy who remembers your middle name is worth two asking whether you prefer princess-cut or round-cut diamonds on the fourth date. Ask yourself, would you rather:

1. Have a guy promise that he's gonna buy you a Range Rover?
   or
2. Have a guy remember that you have a presentation at work and ask how it went?

1. Have a guy suggest moving in together after two weeks of dating?
   or
2. Have a guy hear you talk about Thai food and take you to a great Thai place on your next date?

1. Have a guy claim he's writing a song about you?
   or
2. Have a guy pick you up from the airport when you come back from a work trip?

On the one hand, sure, the big hopes and dreams are exciting and fuel the fantasy of happily ever after, but when they aren't built on a foundation of actual experiences and getting to know each other, each promise is like a hit of heroin (I imagine): a quick high, followed by a big comedown, and then an immediate itch for more.

On the other hand, those reasonable, realistic tokens of affection and attention are like going to bed early when you're really tired instead of staying up late watching TV. It feels good in the moment *and* carries over into the next day. Saying he's going to whisk you off to Mexico might give you heart eyes, but taking you to the movies, dropping you off at home, and texting you afterward to say he had a good time? That's worth its weight in gold.

> **THE SHIFT:** Fantasy building ⟶ Foundation building

Again, I have to acknowledge that yes, there are those rare instances where a guy has told a girl he's going to marry her on the first date and now they have three kids and a French bulldog. Congratulations, we all hate you. Meanwhile, the rest of us are dealing with an epidemic of love bombers telling us they're gonna take us to France when they don't even remember what we do for a living. We need a German shepherd with a good nose.

In terms of how to guard against love bombing: I've said it before, and I'll say it again. Actions speak louder than words. It's easy to say "I can't wait to take you to dinner here" or "We should totally do a weekend trip there" but is this person following up and making plans? If you can't show receipts, run for the hills because this dude's carrying explosives.

> **THE SHIFT:** But he said "____". → What has he actually done?

Lastly, I would like to remind you that when someone says something, they aren't signing a contract. Words are just words and until they are backed up with action, they don't mean anything. See through the smoke. Build a foundation. You're a bombshell and don't you forget it.

CLOSING CEREMONIES:
HOLDING FUNERALS

"You know what they always say: you can't
spell 'funeral' without 'fun.'"

—Unknown

We are gathered here today to pay tribute to the life of a relationship that ended too soon. In fact, it never started. Nevertheless, there is loss, grief, and pain. We mourn what could have been but what never was. Let us join hands and sing that Calvin Harris song that was playing when he ordered you a drink, and then let us never listen to it again. Let us take a moment of silence to acknowledge the two weeks wasted on someone who drunkenly confessed that he was looking for his soulmate, got really sweaty during sex, and then never texted again. Let us know in our hearts that while the relationship has passed on, we are still living, and our task is to live fully and find someone worthy of our greatness. Grant us the peace that this asshole could not give us, and the respect we are owed.

Ashes to ashes, dust to dust.

Here's a scenario: Let's say you are stuck on a guy who ghosted you after going on three mediocre dates. Or a dude who mentioned that your friend was hot and asked if she was single. Or even just a nice but lazy guy who isn't putting enough effort into the equation. As women we waste so much time on people whom we've never *actually* dated. Which further delays being able to meet someone who is *actually* worth our time. We need something significant to help us move along and symbolically turn the page. With that in mind, I invented this mental trick to get over someone who doesn't deserve you. It might be silly but sometimes that's what you need to knock yourself out of a funk, reframe the narrative, and not take something too seriously.

Disclaimer: This is not for long-term relationships, or someone who was actually your boyfriend—that's a whole different process we'll cover in Part 2. This is for guys who held more real estate in your mind than the time you actually spent with them warranted. This is for when it's time to hold a gorgeous memorial and lay them to rest.

Without further ado, here's how to hold a funeral:

1. Treat yourself to an extra-fancy oat milk latte and a manicure or fancy skin product.
2. Put together a playlist of funny and/or sad songs (my funeral playlist consists of playing Jeff Buckley's "Hallelujah" on a loop).
3. Invite a friend over to watch a rom-com.
4. Split a bottle of wine.
5. Review your ick list and remind yourself that he was not, in fact, perfect.
6. Give the guy a eulogy.
7. Allow your friend to tell you why he's actually lame.
8. Refresh your crush list.
9. Take a hot shower or a nice bath to cleanse and prepare yourself for the next exciting phase in your life.

Remember, you want to really go all in on the day of the funeral, but here's the thing: You get ONE DAY. After that he is dead. Gone. Prayers up, fly high, king. He is no longer with us. You have to think of it like you're forming a new neural pathway. Every time you have a thought about him you have to say to Mr. Brain, "STOP!" Hit ctrl + alt + delete and replace that thought with a new circuit. You can choose from any of the following:

- Not my guy.
- I deserve someone who makes me feel my best.
- Something better is coming.

> **THE SHIFT:** But we could have been so great together → I'm sorry for his loss; may he rest in peace

My last bit of advice on man-morial services is that there is no such thing as too ridiculous. The sillier the better. I love getting photos from other women showing me an altar of candles strewn with fake flowers (no real ones, because don't forget it was never a real relationship). I guarantee that even if you are cackling over what a fool you look like, it will one hundred percent help you move past the not-so-dearly departed. Holding funerals frees yourself up to make room for something better—or at least an *actual* relationship, which brings up its own bag of issues. Grab another drink (you'll need it) and let's head to the next section.

PART 2

TOGETHER AND APART

(COUPLING UP, BREAKING UP, AND GETTING OVER IT)

BOYFRIENDS:

WHEN YOU KNOW, YOU (DON'T) KNOW

> "If you treat the wrong person like the right person,
> you could well end up having married the right person
> after all. It is far more important to BE the right kind
> of person than it is to marry the right person."
>
> —Zig Ziglar, *Courtship After Marriage*

Let's say you've gotten past the matching/texting/first date gauntlet. You've avoided getting stuck in the talking phase. You are full-on dating someone whom you really like. First of all, yay! This is such a special time and one you should revel in. Until you realize you've just made it to the next level of hell: not knowing whether he's your capital-B boyfriend. Or if that's what you're even ready for.

Here's my stance: *Someone worthy of being your boyfriend should be someone who brings a net positive into your life.* If it's equal parts crazy passion and hesitation/ambivalence (or worse), that's not boyfriend material. A boyfriend should only make your life better. Less stressful. A *lot* happier. It should not be a deal in which you have to sacrifice any other part of your life. In fact, it should actually spill over into your work, family, and friendships in a good way, allowing you to bring your best self to every aspect of your world.

I know these are all very lofty goals and aspirations, so let me also add that boyfriends can prove themselves in the smallest of ways too. Do they text you when something funny happens? Or vice versa, are they the first person you think of when something hilarious happens to you? Any fool can take you to a fancy dinner, but do you have fun just chilling on the couch with him? For me, the barometer is whether I want him to come along in the car to run errands. I absolutely love car time and I know a guy is right for me if he makes me want to share that with him—even if it's just a trip to CVS.

Once you know you want to forgo your extremely hot and viable singleness for a guy, the next hurdle is not freaking yourself out about the relationship. I know, I know, Miss Future Trip herself shelling out this advice. But because this is my kryptonite, let me tell you from experience that the best thing you can do is to adjust your mindset; instead of wondering about whether you'll be together forever, stop and be present. Enjoy the honeymoon phase. And for the love of God please don't get in your head about whether your boyfriend will suddenly stop liking you. Even if he is super fucking hot and you're secretly wondering how you snagged him. Think of it like landing a great job—they didn't hire you as a favor, they thought it would benefit them too. You were the most qualified candidate for the job.

Again, let me be clear: When it comes to getting ahead of yourself in a relationship, I'm not only the president, I'm also a client. A huge unlock happened for me when I started examining my relationships in terms of how I was being treated and whether my partner made me want to be better in other areas of my life, not just with things that would benefit our relationship. I'd been with guys in the past who were so fun, whom I really got along with, and who were genuinely good people, but if I'd asked myself whether they were pushing me to actually become *my* best self, it would've given me pause.

Not to say you can't be with someone you simply love going out with or who makes you laugh till you cry, but something I wish I would've discovered sooner is that if your partner doesn't also encourage you to grow along with the relationship, you might get tired of the wild nights, or eventually not find their jokes quite as funny. If your friends and family are as excited about your relationship as you are, that's a good sign. If you're even more motivated at work and your man supports your career goals, that's a stellar recipe for success. *If you have dreams you're pursuing that don't revolve around being this guy's girlfriend, it will actually make you a much better partner in the long run.*

THE SHIFT: Will we stay together forever? ⟶ Am I able to be my best self in this relationship?

Last but not least, never forget that being in a relationship is not a win-or-lose situation. *The secret to not messing up something new and exciting is to stop thinking about it as something you can mess up!* Instead, view it as a way to learn about yourself, and hopefully feel supported and uplifted by someone else in the process.

INVESTMENT STRATEGY FOR RELATIONSHIPS:

STOCKBROKER VS. VENTURE CAPITALIST APPROACH

"When people show you who they are,
believe them the first time."

—Maya Angelou

I lived in the Bay Area for eight years, and I met a lot of venture capitalists—VCs, as the Silicon Valley crowd says. You could always pick them out in a crowd of standard-issue tech bros because they had a different energy about them. They were imaginative and open-minded, always seeing what *could* be. Willing to take a meeting with just about anyone based on the *chance* that they'd discover a promising start-up that might be the next big thing. You know, glass-half-full types, but in this case the glass is frosted platinum and they're drinking filtered water harvested from melting icebergs and every bottle purchased helps build floating solar-powered igloos for polar bears.

What I've discovered is that women date just like venture capitalists. We see a guy and say to ourselves, hey, if he got a better job and a haircut and his own place, you know, in three to five years, I can really see this becoming something I'd want a piece of. And then we gather our friends—the board members, if you will—and make sure we have their vote. But in the board meeting, we refine (and perhaps embellish) our pitch. We bring up only the most flattering Instagram photos, scrolling through the unfortunate ones to finally find one from five years ago where he looks better than he does in real life. We get sign-off from the rest of the board and then take a chance based on potential return on investment.

Men, however, date like stockbrokers. They see what's in front of them. They look at their portfolio of options and make decisions based on the day's activity. They notice a girl and what she looks like in that very moment. They consider how she makes them feel that day. When they go to show their friends her Instagram, they pull up the first photo and hand the phone over. They don't say, "She's got a lot of potential." They say, "She seems fun."

I'm no certified financial advisor but I do know that sometimes you need to take the bigger risk to get the bigger reward. VCs make a shit ton of money, and if their instincts are right, they get to see something grow from a glimmer of an idea to a unicorn. But for all the wins they get, they inevitably lose a lot in the process. Meanwhile, stockbrokers don't get a free pass either—they can get blindsided by dips in the market that they didn't see coming, or they might miss out on shares that had low value and then shot way up.

Neither approach is right or wrong, but I think it would behoove women to date more like stockbrokers. Our biggest mistake is the idea that we can get with a guy and mold him into what we want him to be. *Can people change? Of course. But it's rare and you shouldn't sign up to be someone's life coach.* Do you think guys sit around and say, "If Rebecca just changed a couple of things, she'd be perfect"? Fuck no! They either want Rebecca as is or they move on. Instead of investing in some future payoff, women should wake up, look at the market, see that the NASDAQ is down five hundred points, and sell sell sell.

> **THE SHIFT:** I can picture a great future with him ⟶ Would I enjoy the present?

WHAT ABOUT WHEN EVERYTHING IS GREAT?

"Do not spoil what you have by desiring what you
have not; remember that what you now have was
once among the things you only hoped for."

—Epicurus

Does it seem like most of the chapters in this book cover things that are confusing, disappointing, painful, or comically depressing? That's because I'm here to give the advice I wish I'd been given, and the only things we typically need advice about are the tough topics. So yeah, there's not a lot of real estate given to effortless dating, relationships that don't rock the boat, and moments of serene perfection. If you're lucky enough to be experiencing a drama-free connection with someone, just stay tapped into how the relationship makes you feel. Check in regularly with yourself but don't look for problems that aren't there. Put this book down and enjoy yourself, girlfriend!

For the rest of us, let's resume.

BOYFRIEND SICKNESS:
THERE IS NO CURE, ONLY CONTAINMENT

"You can't set yourself on fire to keep someone else warm."

—Unknown

Not many people know this, but in addition to being a devoted mother to my cats, Ceviche and Miso, and an unpaid ambassador for the frozen yogurt industry, I also dabble in infectious disease research and have done extensive analysis that has yet to be reported in a medical journal (so I have no choice but to publish my findings here). In my studies I've discovered a very serious disease that I've named Boyfriend Sickness. It's an aggressive affliction that causes you to lose yourself in a relationship and, worse, lose friends and family by prioritizing the relationship above all else.

Here are the facts:

1. It can be fatal (to family bonds and important friendships).
2. It affects women much more seriously than men (most men are immune to the hetero male variant, Girlfriend Sickness, and even when they're infected their symptoms are generally mild).
3. It tends to affect first-time relationshippers who may have a previous history of chronic singleness.

The severity can range drastically, from mild cases that are nothing more than a nuisance to extreme cases that can drastically alter your life. In its worst form, it can cut you off from your own feelings and values, change your personality, and make you vulnerable to other conditions, including depression, loss of self-esteem, and utter isolation.

Now, it needs to be said that it's totally normal to get wrapped up in a new relationship, and I don't think there's anything wrong with that! Being drunk in love is one of the best feelings in the world. But what's not okay is abandoning the friends who have stood by you through the duds. Ditching the Sunday night movie ritual you've had with your girlfriends since college because your boyfriend wanted to lie on the couch and watch football with you is a shitty friend move—but there's something more insidious that happens too. A bad case of Boyfriend Sickness takes your personhood away and can steal parts of you that you just can't get back.

Since there is such a wide spectrum of effects, I've developed a diagnostic tool to identify the level of infection on a scale of 1 to 10:

LEVELS 1–3:

- symptoms: adopting boyfriend's likes and interests as your own; texting boyfriend constantly when in the company of others; starting sentences with "Brad says _____," "Brad loves _____ too!" or "omg that reminds me of when Brad _____"
- treatment: typically resolves itself with lighthearted teasing from your friends and hearing your boyfriend poop for the first time

- prognosis: similar to the common cold, likely recovery with no long-term effects

LEVELS 4–7:

- symptoms: canceling on your friends to do absolutely nothing with your boyfriend; straightening your hair every day even though it takes hours because that's how your boyfriend likes it; exclusively using "we" statements
- treatment: one or two girls' nights out; an honest heart-to-heart with an understanding but no-bullshit friend; reconnecting with a non-boyfriend-related interest (e.g., pottery, Pilates, volunteering)
- prognosis: with assistance, a full recovery is possible but will likely leave minor scarring on job/social life/dignity

LEVELS 8–10:

- symptoms: actively turning against your friends; getting defensive in the face of others' concern; insisting that your loved ones are being unreasonable/jealous/critical and that your boyfriend is just "misunderstood," or, alternatively, constantly apologizing but not changing your behavior
- treatment: read every book on codependency you can; apologize and make amends; reevaluate your values, needs, and day-to-day habits
- prognosis: could be terminal if serious intervention is not applied but small steps are sometimes a more approachable way to recover; some relationships will not survive the ordeal

The reason I know so much about Boyfriend Sickness is that I got one of the worst cases on record in 2016. Thankfully I recovered from it, but I do suffer long-term effects to this day. I've also lost several friends who caught Boyfriend Sickness themselves and it still makes me sad. The worst part is that it is a preventable disease—we simply lack the understanding and education around it.

The first step in eradicating Boyfriend Sickness is removing the stigma, which is tough because there is so much shame surrounding it. I know just as well as anyone. And okay, yeah, I'm obviously doing a whole shtick here with the disease metaphor, but it's because I'm actually scared as fuck to confess my very real experience with it. This is without a doubt one of the hardest chapters for me to write, and something I've never really discussed publicly (or even privately). Partly because it's embarrassing, partly because I'm afraid of my followers finding out about this period in my life that is so counter to everything I stand for. But in the name of helping other women avoid what I went through, here goes . . .

I got Boyfriend Sickness from a man we'll call Marc when I was twenty-four. We dated for a little over two years, during which I slowly changed who I was in order to please him (it never worked, but how I tried). The sickness crept in slowly, until I was in so much pain I couldn't see clearly. I lost friends, I lost myself, and I lost two years of my life that I can never get back. I can honestly say it is my only regret.

Here's how it happened: Marc was French, and insanely suave. I had graduated college with the idea that now I needed to make over my life into something very fancy and adult-like (instead of recognizing that I was still so young and way too broke to afford anything close to the lifestyle I fantasized about).

I had Reverse Box Theory'd Marc before we even met when a friend told me on a girls' trip, "Oh, there's this guy in San Francisco I used to be obsessed with. He drives a motorcycle. He's French. He wears a leather jacket. He works in VC." Mind you, she didn't say anything about him being kind, or sweet, or funny. But I elevated him to God status. I literally thought this man was the coolest, smartest, sexiest thing on earth, before I even laid eyes on him. I put him on the biggest fucking pedestal you've ever seen in your life. And thus I made myself vulnerable to the worst form of the sickness. Because when you Reverse Box Theory a loser named Chris who doesn't deserve it, that's one thing, but when you put a bad, manipulative person on a pedestal, the result can be very dangerous. This is a cautionary tale I wish I didn't have to tell, but let my tragedy be your warning.

After I heard about him on that girls' trip, my friend ended up connecting me with Marc and we set up a date. I was so nervous the entire day leading up to it, and when I finally met him, he totally lived up to the hype I'd already given him. He was mysterious and quiet and charming, and in a town of dudes who worked at Twitter and wore fleece vests, Marc had this European sophistication that reminded me of the side of myself I'd left behind in the UK. Suddenly I went from being happy with my nice comfortable life of eating rotisserie chicken from the grocery store and going out in the Marina to feeling like there was a whole other world I was missing out on and Marc was my ticket into that scene.

He took me to this bar called Chambers and we had a

bunch of drinks and kissed at the end of the night. And then after the date, he dropped completely off the map. Not one text. I was beside myself wondering what I'd done to fuck it up. Then after exactly two weeks, he randomly emailed me "dinner 7pm." I ignored the glaring red flags of manipulation and same-day date plans (a cardinal rule! that I made up!) and leapt at the chance to see him again. He later told me that he had ignored me for two weeks on purpose to "hook me." And thus began an entire relationship based on a never-ending cycle of his exerting control over me and my bending over backward for his approval.

Boyfriend Sickness snuck in slowly, but there were very clear early warning signs that I ignored. I stopped highlighting my hair because he didn't think it looked classy. I started dressing how I thought he wanted me to dress. After we'd been dating a couple of weeks, I was planning a big dinner at this super-fun place called AsiaSF for my birthday, and I could not for the life of me get him to confirm whether he was coming or not. (Yes, you read that right: The Tinx who tells you all to decline same-day plans was eagerly awaiting the news of my new boyfriend EVEN ATTENDING my birthday dinner.) The restaurant called to confirm my reservation and I tap-danced through my reply with a "Yes! Party of twelve! I mean, I am pretty much a hundred percent sure it'll be twelve, so yes. Will I be charged if it's not twelve? Actually never mind, it'll totally be twelve. Haha, yay!" At the very last minute Marc asked if he could bring a friend, by which I mean he told me he would only come if he could bring his buddy. They showed up late and didn't talk to anyone.

At the time I thought, no biggie, we just started dating, and

I guess I am asking a lot of him to show up to a thing where he doesn't know anybody. But now? If any of my friends or followers described the situation I would gag on my turkey wrap. For the record, the first time you bring a guy around your friends and family is a hugely important litmus test of whether he's a real one. Marc's attitude toward my birthday dinner wasn't a product of early dating awkwardness, it was indicative of a lack of respect for me, and a dysfunctional dynamic that would play out over and over, and progressively get worse. At the time, I constantly convinced myself that it was normal. Looking back, I literally cannot recognize the person I was with him.

Here are just some of the things I did over the course of our relationship:

- I did his laundry (not that this is inherently bad, but it was coming from a place of fear that I wasn't living up to his standards).
- I woke up early to make him a hot breakfast (which would then make me late for my own job). Then he would text me what he wanted for dinner while I was still at work. It was always something elaborate like short ribs, and I couldn't just go to Safeway, I'd have to schlep to three different butchers and then spend four hours cooking dinner *and* dessert.
- I switched cars with him (he had a tiny smart car, I had an SUV) because he had a longer commute and he reasoned that "it would be so fun for me to drive the little smart car." For the record, this would have been fine if we were in a loving relationship, but he was just using me for the nicer ride.

- I paid for everything even though he made triple my income, including a trip to Mexico where I got food poisoning because he Anthony Bourdained me and ridiculed me into eating some highly sus street food. Then he went sightseeing without me while I disposed of my insides at the hotel (which my mom had to book for us last minute because he thought it was "lame" to book ahead of time).
- I accepted that he didn't "believe in" gifts even though I love thoughtful presents and consider them a very important symbol of gratitude. So I went two Christmases, two birthdays, and two Valentine's Days without a gift (which might not be a problem for someone else, but they're a love language for me so this was essentially ignoring a core need of mine).
- I allowed him to move into my room, which I continued to pay all the rent for, because he didn't want to pay rent on his place anymore (regardless of point above re: his making more money than me!).

Pretty cringe, right? I wish I could end the list there, and to be honest I almost did. But there were also more troubling things that happened, things that are hard to admit and haunt me to this day:

- When he texted me from work what he wanted for dinner (always a complicated and involved recipe) and I dutifully made it for him, he would rate what I had cooked for him—which often took me half the day and annoyed my roommates, who had to forfeit their

kitchen every night for my personal version of *Chopped*.
I went from being a normal twenty-four-year-old who
grilled chicken on my George Foreman Grill to suddenly
making *poulet à la moutarde*. (I think I'm beginning
to understand why I now only eat wraps and drink
smoothies in my car.)

- He had an air of superiority about him and acted like
everything I loved was "silly"—my music taste was bad,
the places I hung out at were not cool, I was "basic"
(which, hello, yes). Before Marc, I was in this happy
postcollege bubble, just a young girl having fun with
my friends, doing SoulCycle, getting sushi on Friday
nights, drinking a bottle of shitty Santa Margherita wine
and going out to Comet Club. And then Marc swept in
and showed me that actually everything about me was
embarrassing.

- Oh wait, there's more! His nickname for me, *nunuche*,
means "idiot" in French. You cannot make this shit
up. He called me fat and told me that he usually dated
models but was making an exception for me.

- He used to tease me that I needed to use Google Maps
to get around. He would turn off the directions in my
car and be like, "Just figure it out." I'd try to turn the
navigation back on and he'd shut it off and say that I
shouldn't be so reliant on technology (lol I make a living
using my phone now, joke's on you). I would inevitably
take a wrong turn and then he'd be like, "Well, now
we're late." And I'd apologize.

- I turned down a scholarship to grad school in New York
because he convinced me that it was just something my

parents wanted me to do and that grad school wasn't necessary (and then I convinced myself that his telling me not to go was a sign that he cared about me).

- A year and a half into our relationship, I asked him if he loved me, and he replied, "There are big loves and little loves"—what the fuck does that even mean?!

- My friends didn't like him, and instead of taking that to heart I abandoned them for Marc time and time again. Once when my roommate's mom was in town I was supposed to come to a fun girls' brunch with her and her mom and all our friends. When I told Marc about our plans, he said, "No, I want to drive to Point Reyes and get oysters." I was so desperate for his approval and uncomfortable leaving him that I didn't go to the brunch, which I still feel bad about. (That is why one of my fundamental rules is to never, ever cancel on your friends for a boy.)

- After bringing Marc on a family vacation, my mom straight-up told me, "This is not your guy. You're not yourself around him. You're walking on eggshells." She was concerned that I was putting so much energy into a relationship that was so clearly making me miserable, and instead of that being a wake-up call, it caused a huge rift between me and her.

These last two items are what I just can't get over. I'm all about living and learning from your fuckups, but I can't "live and learn" away the way I acted toward the people I loved the most. I remember seeing Marc be blatantly rude to my friends and making excuses for it in my head. And then when they rightly told me they didn't like him and that he was taking advantage of me, I retreated further into my sickness. It ostracized me from my entire social circle. I stopped getting invited to things because I never said yes anyway.

You might wonder how I could have stayed in this relationship so long, and I don't think I'll ever be able to properly answer that question. All I can say is that the more the reality of the situation presented itself, the more I clung to the story I'd told myself: That I had a cool boyfriend. That I was lucky. My life looked pretty perfect (on Instagram). I'd tell myself that it wasn't that bad because we didn't even fight, when the reality was that the reason we didn't was that I was too scared to argue with him. The person I was in this relationship runs so counter to everything I stand for now, and I suppose it's because I've seen what life is like at the other end of the spectrum. I dated as a means to an end, my sole goal being to get his approval. I gave up everything that gave me joy. I was a terrible friend.

Honestly, I needed The Shift so much in that moment. I never once thought, "Am I my best self around him?" Or even "What do I like about him?" Instead, I thought about all the ways I could shift *myself* to make him happy, and wouldn't you know it, I woke up in a deep depression every day. I felt broken, like a shell of my former fun-loving self. I was exhausted all the time.

Thank God I reapplied to grad school and got in a second time (*without* a scholarship, because they were like "the FUCK we are going to give you money again when you turned us down the first time!"). I left my job at Gap and went to New York. Marc and I must have both known our time was drawing to a close because beyond making some vague plans for him to come visit, we didn't even really discuss what this meant for our relationship, whether we'd be long distance or what. I'd been gone a week, which was the longest I'd been apart from him since we'd gotten together, and realized I was the happiest I'd been in years. We hadn't even talked in a few days, so I texted him, "How are you?" (Let me remind you, this is my boyfriend of two years and I spoke to him like he was a work colleague.) The rest of the conversation went like this:

Marc: Great. Just played tennis and swam. How are you?

Me: Sounds lovely. Are you still planning on coming to New York?

Marc: Yes, but likely after this work thing.

Me: Okay, is something wrong?

Marc: Not really, nice to get some space though.

Me: Between me and you?

Marc: yea

Me: I figured as much, are you wanting to take a break?

Marc: maybe. You?

Me: I'm not sure. It felt nice to have a quiet few days.

Marc: Me too. So let's try it and see.

Me: Until when? I guess I don't really believe in breaks. But for some reason, it feels like the right thing to do. I don't suppose you'd pick up if I called for just a second.

Marc: [no response]

A couple of days later, I was on my way back to San Francisco and I asked him to park my car (MY car!) in my neighborhood and put my key through the porch door. When I got back to my car, it was parked illegally and filled with trash, and our front porch had been wrecked—the wreath ripped from the door, a flowerpot pushed over, just a total mess. The saddest part was that I know he wasn't upset we were breaking up, because I truly don't believe he ever really cared about me. He was throwing a tantrum simply because he wasn't in control of me anymore.

Finally free of the relationship and recovering from the sickness that had held me captive for so long, I was able to take stock of how low I'd gotten. At first, I didn't even know what to do. I'd become a hollow person. It took an entire year to relearn who I was, what I liked, and how to be happy on my own. I was so angry and disgusted with myself and made a promise to never lose myself in a relationship ever again. Thankfully, my family and friends stuck by me and showed up for me (they were probably just relieved they didn't have to see the douchebag ever again). Just like in every other tough moment in my life, I came back to what grounds me the most: surrounding myself with female friends. They literally brought me back to life.

Which brings me to one of the most important lessons in this book: *Boyfriends come and go. And you might even end up marrying that guy you just started dating, but guess what? Husbands come and go too! You know who doesn't? Your ride-or-die bitches.*

I heard JLo speak at an event once (I know, peak life moment) and she said something along the lines of: "You'll fall in love, you'll get married, you'll have kids. I've done all those things. But the people who are with me right now are my mom, my best friend, and my makeup artist." Now, that last person on her list might not be a hundred percent relatable, but can't we all agree that in terms of reliability, it's basically death, taxes, Mom, and bestie?

I'm not trying to endorse a fatalistic view toward love and marriage. And not every boyfriend who sets off a case of Boyfriend Sickness is a villain or a monster. If your first boyfriend in your early twenties ends up being the love of your life, then I'll be the first to sob over the video of him doing your hair in the retirement home fifty years from now. But odds are that the dude you date when you're twenty-three is probably not even going to be your boyfriend by the time you're twenty-five. So if you start ignoring your friends' calls and fail to sustain those relationships, what happens when he cheats on you or you find out you guys aren't on the same page about big life stuff or you just get bored? The fact is that while there is no guarantee in romance, you can usually bet that your best friend will be there with a bottle of wine and plans for some sketchy revenge stunt if needed—but only if you've kept that friendship alive too.

That's why Boyfriend Sickness is so dangerous and why we need to do everything we can to prevent it in our own lives and others'. If you are worried you've caught a case, I have some questions for you:

- Do you feel like you need to hang out with your boyfriend anytime you and he are available?
- Do you feel nervous when you choose to do something that doesn't involve him?
- Do you feel anxious being around your boyfriend and your friends at the same time?
- Have you changed your likes and dislikes to align more closely with his?
- Have you changed the way you dress or other aspects of your appearance based on his preferences?

- Have your friends or family made little comments to you about not seeing you anymore or the effect your boyfriend has had on you? Instead of taking it defensively, could you consider that they ultimately want the best for you? (And if they've had the courage to make a tiny remark, rest assured there's probably much more they aren't saying.) It might not be what you want to hear, but I promise it's not because they want to hurt you.

If this is all ringing a bell, first off: Don't be too hard on yourself. This is a no-judgment zone and I sure as hell am not going to sit here calling the kettle black. The bad news is that Boyfriend Sickness can happen to anyone, but the good news is that once it's detected, the treatment is clear: It's time to connect back to your squad. This doesn't even necessarily mean you need to break it off with your man, but gauge his reaction when you shift your behaviors and if he isn't supportive, it's time to really examine that relationship. Because the issue here is that when you catch a case and are in a healthy relationship, you can generally bounce back, with the help of a partner who encourages the other interests and support systems in your life. But if your relationship and specifically your partner have some preexisting conditions (narcissism, manipulative tendencies, addiction), then it becomes a slippery slope that is nearly impossible to get a handle on. Instead of helping in your recovery, they exacerbate things even more, weakening your immune system and driving a deeper wedge between you and your friends and family.

Bottom line: If he's one worth keeping, he will encourage

you to foster the bonds that were there before he came along. Besides, if he's really the shit, you need to keep him on his toes! The ultimate irony in Boyfriend Sickness is that it ends up self-destructing your relationship, taking away the energy you initially brought into the picture when you had a vibrant network of friends and interests, and replacing it with a draining demand for all of your needs and all of your worth to come from one person. *If you actually care about your boyfriend and want to stay with him, it's that much more important to invest in your life beyond him.* So don't stop going to your book club, don't give up SoulCycle. Nobody has kept a man sitting at home like a house cat. Absence really does make the heart grow fonder and when your calendar and interests are more well-rounded, you bring more to the table for him to be obsessed with. *Sometimes the sexiest thing you can say to a guy is "See you tomorrow."*

> **THE SHIFT:** I love him so much it's hard not to spend every second with him! → It's important to keep investing in other aspects of my life so I can bring my best self to the relationship

If you're on the other end of exposure and Boyfriend Sickness has claimed one of your friends, it's important to tailor your approach to the level of severity you're dealing with. For a mild case and if you genuinely think she's with a good guy but is just clearly dick whipped, some light teasing about how much you miss her or calling her out when she's glued to her phone in your presence ("Earth to Bianca!") can be all it takes to clue her in and nip the infection in the bud. For more serious cases, you really need to be intentional and direct in your approach. Assume you have one shot to inoculate her. Make in-person plans (kidnap her and throw her in a van if needed) and have a conversation in which you let her know how happy you are that she's happy but that you miss her friendship. Do NOT make it about how you feel about the boyfriend (even if he is a total fuckwad). Honestly, you don't even need to mention the dude. Make it about how your friend has changed, how she is not acting like her wonderful true self, and how much you value the connection you two have.

> **THE SHIFT:** My boyfriend is my life, but my friends are resentful ➞ My boyfriend didn't change my life! But he made it better

In closing, I just want to reiterate the importance of this time in your life, and as someone who wasted two precious years of it (technically three, if you count the year of recovery post-breakup), I don't want you to do the same. I would give anything to go back in time and spend those years having fun with my friends, going to grad school a year earlier (and not having to pay for it!), and enjoying single life instead of spending all my energy desperately clinging to the idea of a boyfriend. The only positive outcome of my Boyfriend Sickness was that it made me hypervigilant toward anything remotely similar. It clued me in to the little internal alarm bells I should've listened to and reminded me to always ask myself whether a guy is bringing out the best version of me. And, last but not least, it gave me heartbreak antibodies, which, as we'll learn in the next chapter, can protect you from much more serious conditions in the future.

HEARTBREAK ANTIBODIES:
BUILDING UP YOUR IMMUNITY

"If you never bleed, you're never gonna grow."

—Taylor Swift, "the 1"

Perhaps I'm a complete psychopath, but I think if you haven't gotten your heart broken by the time you're thirty, you're doing it wrong. If dating is a numbers game and you have to play to win, you also gotta rack up a few losses along the way to get a championship ring. (Will I ever learn to stop using sports metaphors?? Stay tuned!)

Just as people who haven't been in many relationships are especially vulnerable to Boyfriend Sickness, those who haven't been exposed to heartbreak and loss can be exponentially more affected by a broken heart. But similar to chicken pox, if you're able to catch a mild case of heartsickness, you are far less susceptible going forward. Whatever you do, don't avoid it until you're a full-fledged adult because if you get it then, that shit will TAKE YOU DOWN.

This is why I say your biggest fear shouldn't be getting heartbroken. It should be losing yourself in a relationship to the point of no recognition. The truth is that Boyfriend Sickness can be far more devastating than an acute case of heartbreak. In one case, you cry and drink some wine and maybe fuck some random but then you're ready to live your life. In the other case, you're stuck in a relationship that slowly sucks the life out of you.

> **THE SHIFT:** Avoid pain like the plague ⟶ Lick the door handle and gather your strength

I think my relationship with Marc and overcoming such a drastic case of Boyfriend Sickness actually made me able to cope with the next major emotional gut punch I went through with a lot more grace than I would have otherwise. (That's for another chapter—the next one, actually.) So I say, build up that immunity, baby. It will ultimately make you stronger.

YOUNG GEMINI:

BETTER TO HAVE LOVED AND LOST

"When someone stabs you, it's not your fault."

—Louise Penny, A Fatal Grace

This is the chapter where I tell you about my ex, commonly referred to on the internet (by me) as YG (aka Young Gemini), which has proven to be really confusing because there's also a rapper named YG. You likely already know that this story ends in disaster. But it was the most perfect whirlwind romance, one that taught me more about myself than any other. So gather round, girlies, and let me tell you a modern-day saga of love and betrayal.

Here's how it all began: I matched with him on Raya, an exclusive, invite-only dating app. Then I saw how young he was (he was twenty-six, I was thirty) and I unmatched him. He seemed like a party guy (pot calling the kettle black again, I know). But we had mutual friends and lo and behold a few weeks later I ended up at a group dinner with him. I'm gonna be honest with you guys, I had had a very fun boozy day in Malibu leading up to the dinner so I was pretty drunk by the time I even got to the restaurant. But I just remember him being the life of the party while also being so in control and confident. All the waiters knew him, he was ordering drinks for everyone. That's about all I remember. Everything after dinner is a blur.

The next day, I was hungover as all hell, but I had brunch plans, so what's a Rich Mom to do? I was so out of my head at brunch I decided I would text YG. Being the sophisticated adult I am, I actually had my friend Livvie send him a message saying, "I'm with Tinx right now and she thinks you'd be really good in bed." Classic move of mine. Hook line and sinker. He DM'ed me so I shot my shot and straight-up told him, "I think you and I should go on a date." He responded immediately, "How's Wednesday at The Nice Guy?" Which we all know is *textbook* plan-making in the Tinx playbook. We were off to a great, albeit alcohol-soaked, start.

That Wednesday rolled around, and I broke my no-dinner-on-the-first-date, two-drink-maximum rule: We spent four hours at the restaurant, had approximately one million drinks, and kissed at the end of the night. He texted me at nine the next morning and said, "I know I'm supposed to wait a while to be cool, but I had such a good time. I want to see you again." He asked to hang out again on Friday and I told him I had dinner plans for a friend's birthday. He said, "Let me take you to Nobu Malibu before your dinner for a snack, like a little happy hour." Obviously I can't turn that down, so on Friday he picked me up (he lived in Venice, I lived in West Hollywood— the comMITment!) and we had a great time again. The conversation was the opposite of superficial—it actually got pretty intense. He told me more about his past, his family. At one point, he kind of called me out in saying that there was a lot more to me than social media showed. I took it defensively until I realized he meant it as a compliment. We just really vibed on a level I hadn't experienced before—we had very different childhoods but had both come out of them knowing exactly what we wanted (and what we didn't want) and our ambitions lined up in a way that felt like together, we'd be this unstoppable power couple.

Eventually I had to get to the birthday dinner, but I ended up seeing him that night after dinner too. The next weekend, we had dinner yet again. I felt like he was texting me all the time. He'd even FaceTime me out of the blue and I'd get so excited. I never worried about what I looked like or felt anxious about where we stood with each other. It was just so comfortable.

The next Sunday he invited me to come to his side of town and took me to his favorite place. That was the first time that we smashed, and I remember that being so intimate with him felt like the most natural thing (even though, if I'm being honest, the sex wasn't great the first time around). He texted the next morning to check in and the conversation was so funny. We felt closer than ever.

We got into this groove of seeing each other a few times a week. It was so refreshingly clear that we were both very into each other. I never felt like I had to draft a text to him in my Notes app or screenshot our conversations to show my girlfriends. I never felt like I had to wait to respond to him. He listened and asked me questions about my day. He was immediately invested in my life and cared about me. We said "I love you" after like three weeks. Readers, it was the fucking best.

The next few months were completely idyllic. He was on my energy level, which I never realized was something I needed. People had always told me that I needed someone calm to balance me out and YG made me realize that I actually thrived being with someone who could not only keep up with me but keep *me* on my toes. I felt very present and in the moment and yet at the same time, it felt a bit surreal, like I was in a movie. There was one particular Saturday when we woke up a little hungover (which we usually were on Saturdays) but decided to rally and go to Venice to meet up with friends. After a few glasses of rosé, we all decided, why not go to this party in Malibu? There's a picture of me in the car going to that party, listening to a song he had put on because he knew it would make me laugh, and I remember thinking to myself in that moment, "It feels illegal to be this happy."

We went to the party and were so lovey-dovey, which is not usually my style, but it felt good to make out with him in public and just put our love on display. Honestly, it felt euphoric. I looked around and realized, I have this great boyfriend, I have wonderful friends, I'm at a party in Malibu on the beach—man, things are going great. I felt really lucky. Thinking about it now, I can still feel the happiness.

Does this all feel like it's too good to be true? Read on!

One weekend, I rented this house in Malibu, and we kind of played house. He drove me extra far to get this special burrito that I'm obsessed with, and then we came back and got coffee and sat on the deck together and it was truly one of the best weekends of my life. It was just so peaceful, and I felt so loved and seen and understood.

What really made me believe in a future with YG was that we integrated into each other's lives right away. He introduced me to the people he worked with, we met each other's friends and would hang out in a big group setting (sidenote: this is always a good sign—you want a mix of one-on-one intimate dates and group hangs to get a proper sense of who the other person is). I loved that he was the leader of his group and was always the one making plans. He had a really eclectic crew and showed up for all of them with so much loyalty. We had only been together a few months, but I was picturing our life together and it just felt right.

Except when it didn't. We ended up getting into a huge fight because YG had heard me on a podcast where I talked about the fact that I had a friend I used to be in love with and we'd still go hiking together. (For more on that, see the Fake Boyfriend chapter.) He had an absolute fit and flipped out for an entire day while I tried to fix things—canceling all my meetings during an important week when I was picking agencies, crying on the phone to my therapist, on pins and needles frantically scrambling to mend things. I should have known something was off. Why was he making such a big deal about this?

The next day we had smoothed things over, and I was hanging with my brother, who was in town from New York. YG called me and said, "Babe, Justin Bieber is doing a surprise performance. I know he's your favorite. Come with me tonight." I didn't want to leave my brother but he told me to go, so YG and I went to the show and I felt almost sick with happiness, being in love and having a boyfriend who could give me such incredible experiences.

We went back to regularly scheduled perfect programming that weekend, going hiking at Runyon, where he stood there and waited while a follower asked me for dating advice, getting smoothies at SunLife, watching TV at his house.

There was a moment that weekend when we were sitting on the couch watching the Kardashian reunion, and Andy Cohen was asking Khloé about the whole Tristan cheating drama. I said to YG, "I cannot believe that a woman in the public eye who'd been cheated on so blatantly could take a man back like that. I would never. Even if I wanted to, I just don't think I could face my followers and the young girls who look up to me." He just sat there in silence. Something in the back of my mind thought, "That's weird."

Not long after that, my manager, Seth, called me, sounding a bit off. He said, "Hey, can you come over?" He was so serious, definitely not his usual self. I tried to brush him off. "Sethy, it's Friday. I'm done working. I'll come over on Monday." He wouldn't listen. "No, you really need to come now," he insisted. Eventually I gave in and left YG's place complaining about Seth being so annoying.

When I got to Seth's house, he sat me down and said, "You told me never to tell you anything about anyone you were dating unless I had proof. And I have proof. Please look through your DMs." I looked at the message he was referring to. It was from a woman saying that she respected me and so wanted to let me know about something that had happened with YG. In her words, she said he "invited me out last Thursday and tried to hook up. I said I didn't think he was single, and he said he was in a 'fake, mutually beneficial relationship.' We made out at Poppy, and I went back to his place." She went on to tell me how grossed out she was by the situation and apologized for her involvement.

I didn't believe it at first. Then Seth brought out the screenshots. Apparently she had sent pics of her text conversations with YG from the week before, on a night when I had stayed in because I wanted to rest for his birthday party the next day. Even more painful, there were texts from him at nine the next morning, asking her to come back over. I thought back to nine o'clock that morning—what was I doing? I was driving to Magnolia Bakery to pick up his birthday cake. Meanwhile he was texting another girl to come *back* over to his place. I was suddenly sick to my stomach.

I felt so devastated because YG had opened up to me about his cheating in his past and confessed that it was a result of his own unresolved trauma. And I knew that this incident wasn't some drunken hookup, it was a pattern of self-sabotage that he'd actually talked with me about but still hadn't been able to avoid—despite the fact that I knew he genuinely loved me. I know to this day that he loved me. I know that the plans we had made together were real, and the vision we had for our future was real. But he just couldn't get out of his own way. He had this terrible habit of testing the waters to see how big of a mess he could make and still get away with it. And it had worked for him in the past, but I had told him I had a zero-tolerance policy. I wished he had taken my word for it and known I was serious. That he would fuck up something he didn't want to lose. I hated that I was the lesson he had to learn.

Needless to say, I was a crying mess. I somehow made it back home because I was supposed to go to a friend's birthday dinner. I was trying to do my makeup but couldn't stop sobbing and had to keep redoing it, over and over and over. I was sitting there in my streaky makeup and robe and thought, "I have a choice." I recorded the first thing that came to mind. When I watch it now, it's actually a pretty incoherent and ploddingly slow video, but I'd been doing TikTok for over a year at this point and had tried to share everything with my followers—even the tough stuff. So I said fuck it. I recorded myself bawling and babbling about what had happened. It was actually my first video that was longer than a minute. Once I was done, I watched it back once and then immediately posted it. I didn't ask my therapist what I should do. I didn't check with my mom or any of my friends. I knew they would all say not to put the video out there, not to air my dirty laundry. But I knew in that moment it was more important to show other women that they shouldn't be embarrassed to get hurt or be vulnerable. Even though I felt humiliated, I wasn't embarrassed that I fell in love with YG. Nor was I embarrassed that I got cheated on. *I wanted everyone to know that when someone wrongs you, it's about them, not about you.*

I somehow pulled myself together and went to the birthday dinner, where my phone lit up with responses pouring in. I had been vague in the video, saying, "If you've gotten one of these DMs you know how bad it hurts," and people thought YG had simply broken up with me over DM, so I clarified that I was referring to a message from another girl. The next morning, I had to get on a plane to go to a wedding (timing—truly a coldhearted bitch). I managed to survive the next twelve hours and flew home on Sunday night in a daze. I decided to go on a solo hike and it was somewhere on the trail, uncontrollably crying, that I stopped in my tracks and said to myself, "Tinx, you still have a choice. You can let this destroy you, or you can put your money where your mouth is and show your followers how to get back on track. You can annotate this heartbreak so it can be used as a guide for people in the future. You can let them see you heal."

I posted (another!) crying video telling my followers that I felt very sad, but that I was seeing this as a rare opportunity to practice what I preach and focus on myself, be a good friend, and drink water (the holy trinity). I said I was going to give myself the day, cry it out, and that the next day I'd make a plan and get through it.

Somehow I was never angry at YG. I suppose I didn't have to be, because I knew immediately I was never going to get back with him. I was just sad because we could have been great together. But I never felt a "fuck you" toward him, I honestly felt sorry for him. I saw his potential and I saw how in every area of his life, he knew what he wanted and would go for it. And this was the one area he continuously fucked himself over. We had a shared vision of what our life could be. It was pretty perfect. Then he ruined it. And that sucked.

But you know what? Despite everything I went through, I'm still grateful for the relationship with YG. Because even though it hurt me in the end, it also showed me that I was capable of real love and commitment. That I actually do want to get married and have kids. This is a huge realization for someone who had previously said she didn't believe in marriage or want a family of her own. Instead of allowing the betrayal to close me off, I chose to allow it to open me up. To take my broken heart and put it back together to be bigger and stronger for the next thing to come along.

> **THE SHIFT:** What did I do to deserve this? → What did I learn about myself?

This is one of the hardest shifts in the entire book to make: to transfer your energy onto yourself and away from the person who hurt you. To know even when you've been betrayed, it says more about the other person than it says about you. And sometimes it can only come with time. (And only if you have a healthy amount of heartbreak antibodies.) That said, it's NEVER easy, and it deserves its own chapter.

LIVING WELL IS THE BEST REVENGE:

THOUGHTS ON CHEATING

"Resentment is like drinking poison and
waiting for the other person to die."

—Unknown

When I was growing up, the big celebrity scandal was Brad
Pitt cheating on Jennifer Aniston with Angelina Jolie. The narrative immediately became a "Jen vs. Angelina" story, painting
them each as part of a Madonna-and-whore dynamic, where
the sweet, innocent Jen was betrayed by the seductive Angelina. You know what headline we never saw, though? "Wow,
Brad Pitt's a Shitty Husband." Never was the focus put on the
person who had done the cheating—it was shifted to pit two
women against each other in some real-life soap opera, plas-
tered across every tabloid with pictures of Jen looking sad or
mad (but still absolutely fucking gorgeous—what a goddamn
goddess).

When I had my very own Jennifer Aniston moment as the
woman betrayed, I made it a point to switch the narrative. First
of all, there would be no angry mob sent to berate the other
girl. Not only that, I didn't want YG to get publicly ripped
apart. And most of all, I did not want my own reaction to come

off as that of the victim, much less as that of someone who had anything to be ashamed about.

Listen, being cheated on fucking sucks. It hurts like a bitch. But it's cut-and-dry. You are in no way at fault. *Cheating isn't something that is done to you, it's something that someone does.* It has nothing to do with you (though of course it can affect you deeply) and everything to do with the person who fucked around. There's nothing embarrassing about trusting the person you love.

Who knows, maybe I'm a toxic optimist, but even after having to tell millions of people that my boyfriend had cheated, I immediately put my focus into forgiving and moving on.

Okay, if I'm being totally honest, I could barely get out of bed for weeks. But I knew my heartbreak antibodies were doing their job and I couldn't allow what had happened to overpower my story. I refused to let it become my identity. Even less than a year after the DM heard round the world, when I think about my relationship with YG, I look back on it as a fond experience. You can take something from every relationship—and I definitely learned some hard lessons—but I would never think of our time together as a waste.

> **THE SHIFT:** I thought he was The One ➝ What did he show me about myself?

If you've been cheated on, I'm not asking you to see it as a good thing, especially in the immediate aftermath. But you need to know that it's only hurting you to hold on to anger. Be as sad as you possibly can, and then draw a line in the sand and say, "Okay, that's that. What's next?"

THE SHIFT: What have I lost? ⟶ What did I gain?

One last thing that helps when you're feeling wronged by someone, especially when you are in payback mode, is to switch from avenger mode to adventure mode. Make them wonder what you're doing. *Living well is truly the best revenge.* Besides, holding grudges gives you wrinkles.

SAY IT WITH ME:

MEN ALWAYS COME BACK OR THEIR LIVES GET WORSE

"But after all is said and done, you're gonna be the lonely one."

—Cher, "Believe"

If you're still feeling petty, rest assured: He'll get what's coming to him.

Let's go back to the Brad Pitt example. He left Jen for Angie, and how did that work out for him? He ended up with like twenty-seven kids, he got divorced again and went through a bitter custody battle, and he has talked about being depressed and feeling alone. I'm not saying he deserved all of that, I'm just saying look at the pattern: A-Rod. Jude Law. Tiger Woods. These are obviously extreme examples, but they underscore an overarching theme: Men always come back or their lives get worse.

Obviously this can give us some small satisfaction when we are recovering from being screwed over, but the more important purpose of this idea is to use it as a tool to shift the energy back onto yourself and away from thinking about him, or wishing ill on him, or, God forbid, stalking his next girlfriend. (Quick note on that, though: If you do end up finding out whom he dates after you and she's some supermodel or cool chef or founder of a badass company, don't let it make you feel small. Think of your ex as an extension of you, and thus their new girlfriend is also a reflection on you. It's like when actors win an Oscar and say, "I'm just honored to be in the same category as my fellow nominees.")

In any case, the best way to make a guy regret losing you is to genuinely not care. When you live your life and are able to move on to bigger and better things, they'll be kicking themselves while in the meantime you've gone and fully forgotten about them. So go on long walks, drink lots of water, work hard at your job, be a good friend, and have fun. *Move forward, not backward.* When you live this mentality, even if he drunkenly DMs you or you randomly run into him, you won't care. (Quick note on that too: If you run into him and, God help you, his new girlfriend, smile, be polite, introduce yourself confidently, and keep it short and sweet. I guarantee they will be more shook than you. And just remind yourself that the reasons you broke up never went away—if anything, have pity on the poor girl who has to deal with his bullshit now.)

> **THE SHIFT:** Ugh, he's moved on! → The reasons why we broke up are still there

There's no way to voodoo or fast-track your way into a guy crawling back. The only way to activate the "men always come back" clause is to truly move on with your life. And just like we learned in Part 1 about breadcrumbing, men have an uncanny ability to only come back at the very moment when you've gotten over them. Don't let it throw you off your game. Instead, when you see him poke his head around the corner, simply nod your head and acknowledge, "Goddamn it, Tinx was right."

THE ROAD TO RECOVERY:
REST, ROUTINE, REEVALUATION, AND REBOUNDS

"Movin' onwards, feelin' strong, but / Healin'
doesn't happen in a straight line."

—Kacey Musgraves, "Justified"

If you picked up this book in a state of emergency and flipped straight to this chapter, first of all, let me say that I'm so damn sorry you're in pain. And since you are reeling from a recent breakup, I will not bullshit you and tell you that there's an easy way to bypass the hurt. The fact is that you're going to be in a pretty huge amount of shock and pain for a few days, or even weeks, because you've been emotionally sucker-punched in the gut. There is no way out but through. That said, there are some remedies that you can use to ease the process.

The first part of the healing journey is to think about a breakup like you're going through an illness. An illness that will definitely kick your ass and wipe you out, but that you will get over with some time and self-care. So take a sick day. REST. You need to reserve your strength. Eat warm and comforting things, preferably delivered to your doorstep. Take care of yourself like you would a child staying home from school. Watch *The Price Is Right* (if that's even still on the air). Eat chicken noodle soup. Keep your Emotional Support Water Bottle (ESWB) nearby at all times (I know I'm a broken record, but crying is mad dehydrating).

Once you've nourished your body, it's time to treat your mind. This is my two-step mental process for successfully getting over a breakup:

1. FIGURE OUT HOW TO GET THROUGH THIS CURRENT PAIN.

You're going to feel a bit wobbly, you're going to wonder what the fuck happened, you're going to feel better for a few moments and try to go out to a party and then randomly start crying at the party. That is all okay. The most important thing is to create a mini routine that you can follow for the next three weeks. Nothing too intense or demanding. It could be going for a walk every day (or even just showering every day) or journaling at night or doing five minutes of leg on wall (see Glossary) in the morning. Commit to the routine and also try to be around friends as much as possible. My friend Livvie has great advice about breakups and the gist is that you have to get it all out with a friend and then you'll have a good six hours of stability until your next flare-up. So whether you need to talk it out, cry it out, or scream it out—just fully let it pour out of you. When I went through my breakup with YG, I'd meet up with Livvie and she would say, "Spit it out." I'd cry for twenty minutes and then we'd have a solid six hours where we could go run errands, go out to lunch, whatever.

2. FIGURE OUT WHAT YOU WANT IN THE FUTURE AND DON'T LOOK BACK. Decide once and for all whether you want to give him another shot or just completely move on. Personally, once someone has hurt me, I can't really go back. But I'm a

cut-and-dry person, for better or worse. If you've made the decision to move on, here's an important shift: Don't make it about "not thinking about him" because that's like the old psychological thing where scientists ask people not to think of a white bear and people's brains are just like "POLAR BEAR" on repeat. If you're focused on what NOT to think about, you can rest assured it will live rent-free in your head. So instead of "don't think about Chris," you need to focus on thinking about YOURSELF. Make this a time to turn inward. (And just as for a person trying to quit smoking it's easier to flush the cigarettes down the toilet than to rely on self-control and willpower, it will be easier for you if you delete his number, unfollow him everywhere, and don't ask mutual friends about how he's doing. Tell them not to say anything to you if they end up running into him or seeing any updates on his social media.) Don't worry about staying on good terms or becoming friends in the future. Is it possible? Sure. But right now? There is no looking back and there is a strict no-contact policy. It will only hinder your progress.

Like I said, while there are no ways to make a breakup painless, there are definitely ways to make it easier, and thus there are also ways to make it even worse. The number one way to do so is to rehash it over and over to get "closure." *Closure is a made-up concept.* We give *ourselves* closure and it definitely doesn't come from unlocking some secret of the relationship or having follow-up conversations beyond the big breakup talk. *The more you try to understand "what happened" the more it prolongs your pain.* Why you broke up doesn't really matter. I know it seems like it does but the truth is simply that ulti-mately, one or both parties didn't see a future in your relationship or want to invest more into it. And that's what you need to focus on. *Not the why but the what.*

> **THE SHIFT:** What happened? → What do I deserve?

Here's the good news: Breakups hurt a lot for a few weeks and then you start to have a shift where you begin to see a ridiculousness that you were too distraught to see before. You can genuinely laugh at the fact that he thought he was the next Mark Cuban. You can be glad that you don't have to deal with his creepy roommate anymore. And you start to feel better. (And that's when they come back. Especially if you broke up for vague reasons or it was sudden. Return to the previous chapter and stay strong, sister.)

Here's a few other things that have helped me:

- Remembering that I have survived a hundred percent of my saddest days before.
- Remembering that heartbreak is something that most people on earth feel at one point or another. This always comforted me. People have been writing books and songs about feeling like this since the dawn of time, and that connectivity is kind of beautiful. The shared universal experience of breakups is part of what makes us all human!
- Realizing that I feel so bad because I am able to love deeply (and not everyone is). So, good for me!
- Trusting that I will love again, and more deeply.

There you go. You have your routine, you have your friends, you have your mantras. But sometimes those things just don't cut it. When all else fails, here are some last-resort methods.

Rebound sex: As long as you're being safe, and as long as you actually feel up for it, I wholeheartedly endorse some rebound sex. Sex after a breakup—particularly a very difficult one—doesn't detract from the healing process, as long as you're doing it for the right reasons. Don't have it because you're still heartbroken and you think it will fix or at least numb the pain. Because then you'll be postcoitally trying to hold back tears while your poor rebound tries to console you. And if you're someone who tends to catch feelings after sex, proceed with caution. But if you're ready to have some fun, do it!

If you feel like you're ready to get back on the horse but feel a bit rusty, know that it's completely normal too. Think of it like going to a new gym—if you've been out of practice for a while, or got really used to your Pilates class, it can be nerve-racking to learn a whole new lay of the land (get it?! LAY!). You build it up in your mind. You know you need to do it, but it feels daunting. Then you do it and you're like, "This is so not a big deal."

Or you do it and you unexpectedly freak out. You have muscle memory of the sex you knew so well in your previous relationship, and navigating a new disco stick has brought up feelings you didn't know you had. Suddenly you're missing your ex. Even if you're fine with the whole "new dick, who dis?" you still have to relearn the art of casual sex, not the kind of sex you have with a long-term boyfriend. There are all these weird moments, like, do you cuddle afterward? Do you nuzzle your head on his chest even though you don't really know what he does for a living?

It's strange. But it's all part of the process. You're learning a new set of wheels, which takes some time but will ultimately make you a more well-rounded person. Have I mentioned I know how to drive stick shift? I had my ho phase in my early twenties living in San Francisco. I was having very good, very casual sex with a few guys I was dating. And I remember thinking, "Well, this is the dream." I felt really good about myself, and I was enjoying it. Honestly, when you're seeing the light at the end of the heartbreak tunnel is a great time to date and hook up, because you're not really looking for anything serious, so your expectations are appropriately low-key.

Or you might want to go the other way . . .

Celibacy: It's like your grandma always said, it's better to have a dry spell than to smash a loser. Having a period of time when you explicitly state that sex is off the table can be a really empowering and clarifying action. You have to rebrand it, though.

> **THE SHIFT:** I'm going through a dry spell ➝ No one's been up to my standards lately

I think periods of no sex can really show you your self-worth. I've gone months without seggs because no one was turning me on. *I've said it before and I'll say it again, women sleep with whom they want to, men sleep with whom they can.* Remember that the choice is yours, and your lack of sex has nothing to do with your desirability, because it's not a matter of someone choosing you, it's you making an empowered choice about the selection out there! And in the meantime, just do what you can to avoid the *Sex and the City* mentality of revolving your life around whether or not you have a man in it. ***Stop defining your worth in terms of whom you are or aren't connected to.*** Instead of chasing a hookup or a relationship or just attention in general, try pursuing *yourself*. This might be the most important takeaway in the entire book: Being alone is a blessing that you don't appreciate until it's gone. It takes a whole lot of mental shifts to be able to see solitude for what it is, which is why I've written a whole damn chapter about it. Proceed!

I'VE HAD THE TIME OF MY LIFE:
AN ODE TO BEING SINGLE

> "Alone time is when I distance myself from the
> voices of the world so I can hear my own."
>
> **—Oprah Winfrey**

So we've acknowledged that breakups are hard. It's impossible not to feel a sense of loss based on the potential you saw in your partner, the plans you had made together, and the memories that now carry a tinge of bittersweet heartache. But the sadness you feel in the aftermath of a breakup should not have anything to do with the fact that you are now single. Because you guys? Being single is actually the best.

I can't stand how society makes it out to be a bad thing, a sad consolation prize and a state that you should try to keep as temporary as possible. I want us all to have a major reframe on how we view singlehood. Because I get that it may seem like a low point when you're in the thick of it. But zoom out to see your life from the thirty-thousand-feet view. When you're able to look at the totality of your story and see its entire arc, you realize that this is actually a period in your life that is precious and fleeting, an era that you won't be able to get back, and one you might even miss.

> **THE SHIFT:** I just want to be in a relationship → The relationship is coming, but I can never get back this time with myself

When I look back on my twenties, I wish I hadn't wasted so much time being sad about being single and instead just appreciated those years as a period of unparalleled freedom and fun. I'd be lying if I said I didn't sometimes have pangs of loneliness, wishing that I had a plus-one to bring to weddings. But then I think about being a hundred years old and looking back on my life, and realize it doesn't make a huge difference if I meet someone at thirty-three vs. twenty-nine.

I just want us all to get away from this perspective that single = sad. No one talks about what you *lose* when you find love—that freedom, that ability to give all of yourself to friendships, creativity, exploration. When you're in a relationship, you have incredible comfort, you have security, you have companionship, but when you're single, you have this incredible unknown. You don't know if your next great love is around the corner, you don't know if you're gonna kiss someone that night. There's a reason that going out is more fun when you're single—it's the *possibility.* *Not knowing whom you're going home with is a luxury that we take for granted until it's not an option anymore.*

Honestly, in my opinion, we have it backward: Coupled-up people are getting the short end of the stick! To really hammer home my point, here's a list of all the things you can do when you're single that aren't as accessible when you're in a relationship:

- Eat a tub of hummus for breakfast, leftover salad for lunch, and an ice cream sandwich for dinner—with no one to judge you or consult with or ask the maddening "What do you feel like for dinner?" question every fucking night.
- Wear the comfiest pajamas and take up the entire bed and have your bedroom be the exact temperature and vibe you like.
- Flirt with the guy at Trader Joe's and give him your number and then actually go on a date and then maybe even fuck the guy from Trader Joe's!
- Fantasize about your future husband (instead of complaining about your actual one).
- Save your money for something you've always wanted (or spend it on an amazing trip somewhere you've always wanted to go).
- Focus on your friendships—including friendships with guys, which can be a lot harder to maintain when you have a man (see next chapter).
- Never watch baseball!
- Make your home your sanctuary with decor that speaks to you and makes you happy.
- Spend more time with your parents or aunts or uncles or grandparents or other family members you enjoy (and who, sorry to say, won't be around forever).
- Grind so hard at work (in moderation, of course—all work and no play makes a burnt-out girlie run down!) and pull some late nights on a special project without anyone bugging or distracting you.
- Focus on your health, go to workout classes, and eat foods that make you feel good.

- Spend time lost in your thoughts, which gives you the space to make breakthroughs and realizations about yourself and the world around you.

Honestly, I could go on. There's so much beauty in being alive and being by yourself. I've had certain days that remind me that it's just about framing. I'll give you an example. One semi-recent Sunday, I woke up, single and untethered, and made plans with my girlfriends Ashley and Daisy. I actually canceled a date to hang out with them. (I just genuinely love them so much. And I was pretty sure I didn't like the guy.) We went to our favorite restaurant, Found Oyster. We had a bottle of orange wine. We were laughing hysterically, fucking around in front of the Scientology building. We went skinny-dipping at my house, and then we watched a movie and got Thai food at Night Market. As I went to bed that night, I thought to myself, "I'm so lucky I have all this freedom." Not to say that a day like this isn't possible when in a relationship, but the goofiness and joy and spontaneity are things I never want to take for granted.

I think the trap that people get into when trying to appreciate being single is that they look at it as an either-or proposition. Either I'm in a happy relationship or I make the most of being single and accept being alone. I don't think you have to separate these two feelings. Of course I want to end up with my person. But what am I going to do in the meantime, not appreciate the beauty that's right in front of me? *You can appreciate the fun that comes with being single* and *still be excited to fall in love.* They're not mutually exclusive.

We need to stop thinking of one versus the other, and we need to start thinking of different seasons of our life. It's like when you were fifteen, you were so eager to get your driver's license. It seemed like you were stuck in some prison, focusing all of your energy on the things you'd be able to do when you had a car, instead of savoring the era of riding around on your bike, getting chauffeured around by your parents.

I'm an advice giver, but I'm also a hard-core advice seeker and taker. And some of the women I most admire, when asked the age-old question of "What advice would you give your younger self?" have said, "I would tell myself to just enjoy it." As someone deathly allergic to wasting time, I think one of the saddest parts of not appreciating being single is looking back and realizing that you've spent your glory days wishing your life was different.

Don't waste this sacred time. Use this period in your life as a chance to reconnect with your friends, go on a trip, go to a restaurant by yourself, stare out the window, have those main character energy moments. You don't know how long this will last, so savor it!

FAKE BOYFRIENDS:

NAVIGATING THE DELICATE BALANCE
OF PLATONIC FRIENDSHIPS

"Can we keep, keep each other company?"

—Justin Bieber, "Company"

I sometimes get called a man hater (usually by insecure men who are threatened by the fact that I encourage women to prioritize their own happiness, but I digress). However, this chapter will prove that, actually, I love men too much. *Especially* when I'm not dating them. There's just this special allure to someone sitting at the intersection of "as fun as hanging with your girls" and "has a penis." They're like a hybrid of the comfort you get from a close friend and the horny sexual tension that happens when masculine and feminine energy come together. It's the best of both worlds, because you get to have male companionship without all the other obligations that come along with having a boyfriend. Think of it like Rent the Runway for men—you get to try something on for a weekend without all the stress of buying it, and then you can return it when you're done. What's not to love?

Like I said in the previous chapter, when you're single, you can hang out with the opposite sex more because we all know when you have a boyfriend it becomes kind of complicated to hang with your guy friends—and when your guy friends get girlfriends they basically disappear. So this is a really special time and a unique bond that you can't have in the same way during other periods of your life.

Now, I've made being a girl's girl my entire personality, but the truth is that ever since leaving the all-girls school environment, I've been obsessed with hanging out with guys. When I went to college, I had this really fantastic co-ed group of friends, the type of friend group that's written about in movies. Ben and Haley were kind of at the center of the crew because they were dating. And the rest of us were able to just party together. We'd go to the dining hall in our pajamas and have spontaneous picnics that turned into spontaneous keggers, and there was this *Friends*-like vibe that can only happen when there's male-female energy. It's no surprise to anyone that I became the president of my sorority, but it was a huge step for me to actually have guys in my life whom I could rely on and relax around. That's really when I fell in love with how comforting, cozy, and reassuring it can be to have guy friends.

When I moved to San Francisco after college, living in the big purple house with Mollie and two other girlfriends and just down the street from four Stanford boys, the dynamic just carried over. We would do big Sunday night dinners and grocery shop as a group at Safeway—nicknamed "Dateway" because it's where all the hot single people in the Marina went. It was the scene for many exchanged numbers between post-sorority girls and post-frat guys with jugs of Carlo Rossi and frozen pot stickers in their carts. We'd make a shopping list and divide and conquer, and my friends would always yell at me because I would open the ingredients and start eating them in the store.

(I now have the decency to wait until I get into my car.) We'd drink wine and roast a chicken and honestly it was the best of times. Those guys felt like my brothers. They gave me a sense of security I craved so much and fulfilled a deep need for intimacy and close connection in a nonromantic sense. Then I got into a terrible relationship with the aforementioned Marc and disappeared for a few years.

After I broke up with Bad Marc and recovered from my Boyfriend Sickness, I went through an, ahem, *fun* phase. I was just getting my groove back after having been knocked so sideways. There was this place called the Battery, which is San Francisco's answer to Soho House. I wasn't a member, but my girlfriend was, and she took me to a party there. The crowd parted and suddenly I saw this guy who looked like he was out of a nineties boy band. He had long, blond hair, the most amazing jawline, and luscious lips. In a city of North Face jackets, there weren't that many guys who actually looked cool, so I went up and introduced myself. Turns out, he worked at Google by day and was a DJ by night (if you know me, you know how I feel about DJs). He was a couple of years younger than I was, which feels like a huge age gap when you're in your twenties. Between that and the fact that I was still pretty fresh off the Marc breakup, I didn't even consider him a serious dating prospect. But we exchanged numbers, texted back and forth, and started casually hanging out. Our "dates" were such a welcome break from my usual scene of going out in the Marina—he'd take me to underground ramen spots, and I'd go to see him DJ at 1040 Folsom. He even took me to the Google holiday party. But we barely hooked up and I referred to him as "Friend." Looking back on it now, I think the reason our relationship worked so well was that lack of pressure and the fact that I didn't Reverse Box Theory him. We just had fun together.

About a year after we first met, Friend moved to LA and I went to New York. I missed that vibe I'd had with him, so I sought out some old Stanford buddies, Jeremy, Neil, and Ben, to go on adventures with. We would go to Queens for dumplings on Sundays and have Friendsgiving in tiny Manhattan studios and get drunk at art gallery openings together. New York was a challenging city for me at that time, but those dudes helped me feel grounded.

Around this time, I started really paying more attention to the nature of my male friendships and the comfort they provided me in times of need. I realized that as I got older, I didn't always want to do shots with my guy friends at the bar, I wanted to get lunch and play a board game. I coined the term "fake boyfriend" to describe the kind of platonic hangout that isn't an actual date but, in some ways, is actually more intimate than a date. Harmless, wholesome, and safe. At least it seemed so at the time . . .

Then, fast-forward to moving to LA and I was alone in a new city again. My friends were all getting married and working successful jobs and I was lost and honestly kind of spiraling. I reconnected with Friend, and we went to what would become my favorite restaurant, Craig's. We sat at the bar, and he told me he had left his job at Google and was now working in music. He was so much happier and seemed like he'd really figured his shit out. I felt so unsure of myself at that time, and he was so supportive and reassuring and promised to give me the lay of the land in LA.

And this, dear readers, is when Friend became my fake boyfriend. He called me when I was in a funk one day and said, "Do you want me to pick you up and we can go get dinner and go to the Grove?" And I replied, "That is *exactly* what I want to do." I hadn't realized how desperately I wanted to get dinner at Joan's on Third and then go walk around the Grove and go to the Apple Store. You know, things you do with your boyfriend. Not a date. Just silly little errands and doing normal life stuff together. Playing pretend with all of the safety and none of the stress.

This became a regular occurrence and I actually started to enjoy myself more in LA thanks to Friend. Of course, there was some sexual chemistry between us, but we didn't act on it. We were just friends! Which made it easier to flirt—playfully, of course! And we'd known each other for more than three years at this point. Which made it easier to just call each other up and hang out without it being a big thing. Then the pandemic hit.

There I was, living alone in my sad studio, not seeing anyone, completely isolated and completely out of my mind. Friend hit me up and said, "Okay, here's what we'll do. Every Saturday, let's go on a hike." So once a week, we'd meet up and go for a walk. In the beginning, it was very short and sweet—we'd meet at the trail, do our little trek, and go our separate ways. But as time went on, the hike often turned into lunch. This was in the days when restaurants weren't open to dine in, so we'd pick up takeout and drive somewhere and eat on the trunk of my car. And then lunch would turn into an adventure to the beach or going to a neighborhood we wanted to check out. And soon we were spending all day together, exploring different parts of LA, finding secret walks and hidden gems. We weren't even drinking or doing anything crazy—just normal things and natural conversation. I felt seen around him. And so, naturally, I started to develop raging feelings for Friend.

I blame it on the pandemic. I had regressed into a very immature mindset in quarantine, which reactivated the crush neurons in my brain and focused all of them on the only guy I had access to at the time, meanwhile ignoring the sage wisdom of Billy Crystal in *When Harry Met Sally* when he said, "Men and women can't be friends because the sex part always gets in the way."

I had forgotten that which no one should forget and I could not stop thinking about hooking up with Friend. So I texted him a classic Tinx line: "I think I'm going crazy because I keep thinking about us smashing." He responded immediately, "Well, should we?" I coquettishly tossed back, "Haha, maybe." And here's where things got hairy.

We made a plan for him to come over later that week. (Keep in mind that I was still living in my cave-like studio apartment that didn't even have a couch—just a chair, a kitchenette, and a bed. I had set the scene more for a murder than some hot romance.) I had probably three drinks before he even got there because I was so nervous, and then when he arrived, we promptly got obliterated. Clearly, we both wanted to hook up, but we'd been such honest-to-goodness innocent friends for so long and had a really nice, casual dynamic together. As a result, we didn't know how to switch on the sexual vibes and had really terrible drunk sex.

For so much of my life, I'd had a lot of anxiety around the morning after. But when I woke up next to Friend we just started joking around like normal and I thought, "Maybe this'll be fine?" I felt more than a little bit weird about it, but he made an effort to be very emotionally mature and addressed the elephant in the room. He told me, "You know, I think the reason it was kinda weird is because we planned it—it felt like we were losing our virginity again or something. Why don't we just sleep together when we feel like it?" I responded that I totally agreed and we left each other feeling like responsible adult friends who had just shagged each other in the most rational way possible.

We continued to talk every day, go on hikes, and occasionally sleep together. And as we became closer friends, I stupidly started to fall even more in love with him. But here's the thing: Sleeping with Friend wasn't the part that made me catch feelings. It was the fact that here was this guy whom I could be myself around, and do my favorite things with, and he was so kind and easy to hang out with (and okay, obnoxiously hot).

This was around the time my TikTok started blowing up, and I had finally really hit my stride professionally and personally. I'd started posting these vlogs, mostly as a way to document what was happening in my life, because between pandemic stress and excessive drinking I could barely remember one week to the next. One day I posted a photo of shirtless Friend from behind on one of our hikes and said, "It should be illegal to have friends this hot." I didn't think twice about it because he didn't have TikTok and I didn't really think anyone else cared much. Then I said something on TikTok the next week about having feelings for a friend. Oh, and while I was at it, I made a playlist and called it "POV: You're falling in love with your friend." TikTok Sherlocks obviously picked up on it and started inquiring and asking for updates.

Since I live in service to my followers, I posted a video talking about how men and women can't be friends, and I'm a fucking idiot because I started sleeping with my friend and now I'm in love with him. Talk about a false sense of security—I could confess this to countless strangers on TikTok but couldn't share my feelings with my friend. Welp, next thing I knew, the video had four million views. All of a sudden the playlist had fifty thousand followers. Meanwhile, Friend had no fucking clue.

In the midst of this fake boyfriend fiasco, I had decided to have a little staycation at the Sunset Tower Hotel because I hadn't been able to travel home to see my family and rooms were really cheap. Friend came to see me, and we ordered food and had sober sex. And it was like, *good* sober sex. I thought to myself, maybe this whole fake boyfriend thing isn't so fake after all?

I should note here that Friend had never been in a relationship in his entire life. He wasn't necessarily a fuckboi but he exuded sex appeal and clearly hooked up with a lot of women. He wasn't the most classically handsome guy, but whenever he walked into a room girls just wanted to fuck him. This had never been an issue for us in the past, and I knew that he was still seeing other people (even though I certainly wasn't because of the whole being-in-love-with-him situation).

Anyway, we went down to the pool and there was a really pretty girl lying out. And I knew in that very moment what I'd gotten myself into, because I could tell they were checking each other out, even though Friend and I were clearly there together. And I had no claim whatsoever. I felt sick to my stomach but didn't have a chance to really process it because suddenly everyone cleared out of the pool area when a kid took a shit in the water. I pushed the discomfort down and bottled it up right next to my one-way devotion.

The next weekend Friend and I were going to Manhattan Beach to visit a friend of mine and as we drove down, he tried to casually bring up a "hypothetical" situation, saying, "If we were out together and um, you saw a guy you wanted to have sex with, you'd feel okay going to talk to him, right?"

I just looked straight ahead and said, "This is about that girl by the pool."

"How'd you know?" he asked.

I ignored the question and just asked him straight-up, "Did you go back to see her after we left?"

"No," he said. "But I found her on Instagram."

You can guess the rest. I was so hurt but also felt like I had no right to be upset. I knew Friend was never going to date me, but I still couldn't shake the idea that we were destined for each other. I decided the only way to get over my fake boyfriend would be to find a real boyfriend.

Brilliant plan hatched, I sounded the alarm to all my friends to set me up with a nice guy—boyfriend material. And boy did they deliver. New Guy was from Santa Barbara, had a great job, was tall and polite. The first time we'd met at my friend's house, he had asked for my number, then texted me later that night and said, "So great to meet you. Do you want to go to Dan Tana's on Thursday? 8 p.m. reservation?" I'm like, fucking perfect. We went on the date, got pleasantly wasted, had a great time. He texted me the next day, still following protocol to a tee. Our second date was—wait for it—a picnic he got from a French restaurant with fancy wine and delicious cheese.

It was like I'd manifested the kind of guy I'd told all of my followers to look for.

I told said followers about New Guy and everyone was rooting for him and he just kept knocking it out of the park. He took me to Hotel Bel-Air for my birthday and got me a Dan Tana's sweatsuit. We had—and I cannot stress this enough—phenomenal sex. New Guy became friends with my friends. It was perfect and sublime, and I just kept thinking about Friend.

Meanwhile, Friend was completely unfazed by my getting a boyfriend. When I bragged to him about New Guy, saying, "Oh my God, he's so great, our sex is amazing," Friend would sincerely respond, "Sick, I'm so happy for you!" My plan wasn't working.

I did everything in my power to convince myself that New Guy was the best person for me, but we inevitably broke up because good on paper just doesn't necessarily translate to the heart. I ended up telling Friend about my feelings, and he wasn't on the same page. Thankfully, it didn't ruin our friendship, and I know I never would have been able to move on if I hadn't confessed, so I don't regret it.

Here's my toxic positivity side coming in again, but similar to how I felt about YG, I actually wouldn't have changed anything about what happened with Friend. It taught me more about the different forms that love can show up in. Friend got me through an incredibly disorienting time in my life and reinforced the idea that relationships aren't a win-or-lose situation and that finding a boyfriend isn't the end goal. We still hang out all the time and I really savor those long Saturdays, because I know that this kind of friendship won't last forever. We will both replace each other with someone else eventually. But instead of being sad about that, I enjoy what we have, bumping around with my fake boyfriend and going on adventures.

> **THE SHIFT:** I must find a boyfriend ➞ I need a friend right now

People often tell me they have feelings for their guy friend and ask what they should do. My answer is always to have an honest conversation about your feelings as soon as possible. Even if it's uncomfortable, even if it changes the relationship. And whatever you do, don't sleep with your fake boyfriend before you have that talk.

That's where I went wrong. I made it so complicated and turned a perfectly good friendship into a friend-with-benefits situation (and brought the entire internet into the fray by vlogging the whole thing). All's well that ends well, and thankfully he is still one of my best friends. But next time, I will focus more on boundaries and less on imagining what his dick looks like.

> **THE SHIFT:** Men and women can't be friends ➞ Enjoy time with your fake boyfriend—just don't fuck him

GIMME A BREAK:

A GUIDE TO DUMPING WITH DIGNITY

"When's the best time to leave? A little before you're ready."

—Tinx Original

Sometimes the hardest thing in relationships is knowing when to call it quits. If the relationship isn't a shitshow, then how bad is too bad? Don't all relationships require work? Some people say that if you're even questioning a relationship at all you need to move on, but I think it's healthy to constantly examine who you are, where your relationship is, and where you want your life to go. As long as—and this is the crucial part—it is followed up by action. Otherwise this kind of mental merry-go-round can help keep you spinning around and around in a stagnant relationship until you can't see clearly. The tricky part is that things are rarely clear-cut and for every reason to leave, there's another to stay.

Not to worry—I have a hack for this! *You don't have to know that you want to end up with someone forever, but you have to know that you want to do the next big step with them.* So say you're dating them casually, you have to want to date them more seriously. Say you're dating them seriously, you have to think, well, I'd like to move in with them. You don't have to know that you want to die with them at age ninety-nine. But do you want to meet their family? Can you see going on a trip with them? Adopting a dog together? Register how it makes you feel physically. I find this trick very helpful because sometimes we really just don't fucking know whether we're with the right person. But this gets you more in touch with how you feel on a basic level. If the thought of future milestones with this person makes you feel trapped—that's a big clue, girlfriend.

The perfect example of this is New Guy, whom you met in the last chapter. He was great. In fact, he was perfect. He took me on the most incredibly thoughtful dates. He called me just to check on how I was doing. He would text me at all the right times and with all the right things to say. One time I was sad and he brought me wine and flowers and went on a wine walk with me. Like I said, perfect. We went away to Palm Springs together. (Here's a tip: If you ever want to get a better sense of your relationship, travel can really bring things into the light.) We were driving there on a Friday night. Anyone who knows me knows that car time is one of my favorite things. Being in the car with a boy, listening to music, is the horniest thing in the world to me. There's just something so intimate and intense about being in the car with someone, never mind looking over at a hot guy driving with one hand on the wheel. The car ride to Palm Springs is one of my favorite drives too—so it was on this car ride that I knew once and for all I had to break up with New Guy. I was just not feeling it. But we were already deep into the drive so I stayed quiet and let the realization sit in the back of my throat. I knew that I was going to have to break up with him at some point in the near future, but I just couldn't bring myself to do it on the drive. So I did what any normal person would do, which was to get completely, like completely, obliterated as soon as we arrived.

The next morning, I was feeling rough. I was kind of a piece of shit all day, just lying in bed, avoiding the reality of the situation and blaming it on my massive hangover. That night I didn't have the luxury of passing out wasted, so I lay next to him, listening to him snoring so loud that I actually went and slept in the basement. He woke up apologizing profusely for the snoring, and by the grace of God I had to quickly go back to LA for a work thing, so I fled in my car as fast as I could and he caught a ride home with friends.

The following weekend was New Guy's birthday, and he had a huge party planned. It was around Halloween, so it was a costume party and he wanted us to dress up as a couple. He kept talking about how excited he was to introduce me to his wider group of friends. And here's the thing: I could've sucked it up for the party so he could have a good time, but I knew that was actually the more cruel thing to do. *Staying with someone you know you don't want to be with is actually deceitful, and being dishonest with someone is more aligned with cheating than it is with doing him a favor.* (Read that again if you need to.)

Don't let timing be your scapegoat. So many women write to me saying that they want to break up with their boyfriend but they have a trip planned, or it's the holidays, etc. etc. But the real truth is that you don't want this discomfort and it feels easier to live a lie for a little bit longer. We tell ourselves we have the other person's best interests in mind, that we don't want to hurt them—but if staying with them is a lie, isn't that far more of a betrayal? Trust me, it's kinder to rip the Band-Aid off and to be resolute about it.

I've made a rule for myself that once I've realized that I don't see a future with someone, I break it off completely within twenty-four hours. For me, it's not just about making the right decision, it's about making the decision right—as in RIGHT NOW. Can I be a little militant when it comes to breakups and not waiting even a day to do it once I've come to the conclusion? A hundred percent. But have I ever regretted breaking up with someone? You bet your ass I haven't. In fact, the only breakup regrets I have are for not doing it sooner. *It's not an impulsive decision when you're following your gut.* And it really doesn't behoove anyone to drag it out while you figure out the perfect exit plan (there is none, babe).

Bottom line: Now when I make a decision, I follow through with it right then and there. I should've broken up with New Guy on the car ride to Palm Springs but I avoided it, thinking I was doing him a favor, when in fact it was selfish of me not to be honest. I am grateful, though, that I at least broke things off before his birthday party. I went over to his house a few days before and gave it to him straight. It was a clean break and the kindest thing I could have done.

In case you ever need to compassionately and respectfully put a relationship to rest, here's the basic script: "I have loved our time together. But I've realized that I don't see a future long term. And I know we're both looking for the real thing. I respect the hell out of you. I also like you so much as a person. But carrying on would be dishonest for me, because these are my feelings."

I told New Guy this, and he took it so well and totally understood. Just kidding—he was incredibly upset! Don't get me wrong, no matter how you deliver the blow, it'll still sting like a bitch. It is a similar feeling to, say, cliff diving nude off a steep ravine into shallow waters. But the temporary discomfort and inevitable pain you may cause is so much better than being wishy-washy. Be direct. Keep it short and then get the hell out of Dodge. Instead of making sure they know how much you really did like them and wish it would have worked out, think about allowing the other person to get over you as quickly and smoothly as possible.

> **THE SHIFT:** I don't want to hurt this person ⟶ I'm going to hurt them eventually

I know this is a particularly tough decision to make when you've been in a very long-term relationship. After all, if you've been with someone for years, there will certainly be rough patches and that doesn't mean you're not a great match. There are definitely moments when you need to tell yourself that things suck in the present moment, but they will get better. However, this is only useful when the shitty things are circumstantial: a family member's illness, a job loss, a baby who refuses to sleep. If you're just feeling a general sense of blah (or worse) about your partner but can't pin it to something outside the relationship, you need to stop looking for a light at the end of the tunnel and ask yourself: How will I feel if things look exactly the same five years from now?

> **THE SHIFT:** Things will get better ⟶ What if things stay the same?

If you've decided that you want to make things work with this person, I fully believe in the power of couples therapy—as long as both parties acknowledge the issue and want to work through it. A lot of people keep their relationship doubts to themselves, further isolating themselves from their partners and sinking deeper into their misery. But I actually think that the couples who are struggling and who come right out and talk about whether they should break up have the best chances of making it work. I'm putting my money on two people who agree to try despite the fact that they're constantly at each other's throats, over the couple where one person is quietly thinking to themselves, "Do I want to be with this person?"

What I really want to help other girls avoid is doing everything possible to keep a relationship going, just for the sake of being in a relationship. Or because of the sunk cost fallacy—the idea that you've invested so much time that you'd rather stay in a dead-end relationship than go back to square one alone.

Age plays a huge role here. It's easier when you're in your twenties to say, "Fuck this, I'm young, I have so much life to live, I don't want to waste any more of my time." But if you're thirty-five and have been with someone for several years, the thought of starting over seems like taking a huge step back. You're watching all your friends get married and have babies and feeling like you need to suck it up or you'll miss the boat. But you owe it to your future self to live the life you deserve, not the one you settle for. Otherwise you'll just put off the breakup from when you're thirty-five to when you're forty or forty-five or . . .

> **THE SHIFT:** It's too late ⟶ You're never too old to become single, if that's what you need to be happy

Here's another way to think about it: Imagine a year from now, you're having drinks with some close friends and they ask you about your life. Do you want to say, "Well, I was thirty-five and miserable but I was afraid to be alone so I stayed in a depressing relationship"? Or do you want to say, "I'd been in this relationship for nine years, I thought I was going to marry him and have kids with him. But I realized he wasn't really the one. So we broke up and it was a fucking shitty six months. And you know, I learned a lot and it was scary. But I had to advocate for my future happiness."

> **THE SHIFT**: I'm unhappy now but afraid to be alone →
> What's the story I'd want to tell about my life?

It is only natural for the idea of starting again to be completely and utterly terrifying. But it's a momentary discomfort for the sake of long-term peace. You don't win a reward for grinning and bearing your way through life. You never hear anyone say, "You know what, I'm glad I toughed it out. I'm glad I stayed in that situation." What happens is you're miserable for six more years, and then you leave. Or even worse, he leaves you. *Because unhappiness is not sustainable.* So if you aren't happy—doesn't matter if you're twenty-one or forty-nine—it's time to make a plan. *You're not too old and it's not too late.*

Here's what you do first: Set a date. Mark it in your calendar and know that by that date, you will have made your final decision and taken the steps to make a change one way or another. It can't be three years from now, but it can be three months from now if that's what feels approachable. The important thing is that you need to have a strict agreement with yourself that you're either gonna work to make things better or you're going to break it off. Write that shit down and commit to it like a contract because otherwise you will get cold feet and might stay stuck in purgatory. And you know what's worse than a breakup? Limbo Land. We always act like the breakup is the pinnacle of devastating sadness, but when you look at it in hindsight, the period *before* you actually split is far worse. The anticipation, the feeling of being stuck. I wasted a year of my life in purgatory from age twenty-five to twenty-six. One of the hottest years of my life! And instead of enjoying it I woke up every morning miserable, thinking, "I'm not going to marry this guy. He doesn't make me happy." ***Breakups are hard but purgatory is soul-crushing.***

If you get to your chosen date and decide it's time to split, you need to rehearse how you'll break the news. If you're fairly young and haven't been together a super-long time, be direct and keep it positive. Here's a rough script: "I need to be really honest with you. I think you're so amazing. And I have a really good time with you. But I don't think there's a romantic connection that can grow, otherwise it would have grown by now. I don't want to waste your time or mine. Thank you for all the good experiences we've had and I hope we can one day be friends because I think you're truly wonderful."

If you have kids, obviously there's a lot more to navigate. Kids are scared of change. And I don't think anyone *wants* their parents to split up. But the thing to remember is that they are kids. And you are the parent. It's your job to know what you're going in with when you tell them what's happening. If you say, "Honey, what do you think about moving to a different country and leaving school and Mommy getting a different job—do you think that's a good idea?" they're gonna be scared and confused as hell. But if you say, "Hey, your dad and I are getting a divorce, and it's gonna be tough for a little while, but I'm gonna figure out everything and we'll always be a family; this is a good decision because I want to be happy and be the best person and mom I can be," there's a much greater chance they won't see this as a moment that ruined their life.

Not to say that it'll be easy. I've heard from women who were in their late thirties/early forties, with multiple kids, who just knew they weren't happy. And they left. And it was hard. And money was tight. Many moms tell themselves to stay in it "for the sake of the kids." I obviously don't have children so I can't imagine what that's like, but let me tell you, as someone who sometimes wished that my parents had gotten a divorce, it's more important for your kids to see you happy than to see their parents together. (See: Glennon Doyle's *Untamed*—she articulates this better than I ever could.) It's so meaningful for your kids to see you advocate for yourself. Because kids aren't stupid—they'll know if you're faking happiness just for their sake. This is an issue close to my heart because I've watched it play out in my mom's life.

My mom grew up in a different generation, where she was never taught to prioritize herself. Boomer women didn't enjoy all the privileges we do today—no therapy (at least not commonly or shamelessly accessible), no body positivity, hardly any resources to juggle higher education or professional aspirations with the demands of raising a family. So instead of making a life she loved for herself, she gave up her own passions, quit her job, and selflessly sacrificed herself for my brother and me.

This isn't to say that motherhood can't be satisfying on its own. It's just about choosing your choice, which is a luxury that older generations of women didn't have. I don't think my mom felt she had any other options to choose from.

She was and continues to be a phenomenal mom. But the unintended effect that this had was that while I saw her model behavior that showed me what a good mother can do, I didn't see what a happy, self-possessed woman who knows her worth looks like.

There's this Carl Jung quote that says the biggest burden a parent can give their child is not living for themselves. You can't shield your kids from the realities in life. What your child actually needs is to see their parent stand up for herself and say, I value myself too much to sacrifice my happiness.

It was only in writing this book and unpacking my own family history that I realized how my childhood planted the seeds for this philosophy that has made me famous on the internet. I mean, everyone is a walking reaction to the way they grew up, so this connection is not shocking. But when I see all of the advice I give to other women as clues to what I wanted in my childhood and how it affects my relationships as an adult, it's like FUCK. It's why I invent rules and find safety and security in acting swiftly and definitively. It's why I didn't even think twice about leaving YG. And it's probably why the relationship with Marc was so damaging, because even with all the defenses I'd built up, I still slipped into a pattern of self-sacrifice and losing myself in a relationship.

This is the reason I feel the need to be so strong in my own life, and for my friends, and yes, even for my followers. I don't just make shit up and tell you to do it—this is where it all comes from. I decided to devote my life to seeking justice and preventing other women from losing themselves, because I've seen it firsthand. That's the rhyme for my reason—I don't just get off on making commandments for girls to follow, it's coming from a deep, deep place. What started as a personal defense mechanism has now evolved into a mindset that can help women in any situation put the focus back on themselves.

And this is why this book's final section is about self. Unlike so many other relationship and dating books, the goal of this one is not to get you to a place where you're happily married. And that's not because I'm anti-men or anti-marriage—quite the opposite. I love men, but my mission in life is to build women up. I do want to be married someday, but until that time I think it's important to focus on myself and know how to be my own person, so that I can enter into that union as an equal partner. The purpose of this final section in the book is to give you the tools so that you don't waste precious years of your life, so that you can have the maximum amount of fun instead of operating from a place of fear and a scarcity mindset, and so you can make this an era of self-discovery and self-knowledge and bring that person to whatever relationship you end up in. If you do this, you will never get lost in a relationship. You've invested too much in yourself.

PART 3

SELF-WORTH AND SELF-KNOWLEDGE

(THE ERA OF SELF-DISCOVERY)

ALL BY MYSELF . . . JUST WANNA BE . . . ALL BY MYSELF

"I'd be quite happy if I spent from Saturday night until Monday morning alone in my apartment. That's how I refuel."

—Audrey Hepburn, *Life* magazine

At some point you have to realize you're all you've got. Of course we have friends and family and dogs and cats and our Netflix queue, but the truth is, we come into this earth the same way we go out: alone. But that thought shouldn't depress you—quite the opposite, in fact. Instead of treating it like an afterthought—or worse, something to avoid at all costs—I want us all to truly understand that the relationship you have with yourself is the most important thing in your life. Nothing else is more meaningful. Not your partner, not your kid, not your job. Your relationship with yourself is the source of all your drive, passion, determination, and ability to love and be loved. On the flip side, it can also be the reason why you can't achieve your dreams or love deeply or even know what makes you happy. ***To bring your best self to dating, you need to focus on self above dating.*** So not everything in this section will be specifically about dating, and that's intentional.

Let's begin with the core problem: Many of us forget that

we can even have a relationship with ourselves. We think re-lationships only count if they involve another person. And the more serious, the more committed, the better. Exclusive beats casually dating. Fiancée trumps girlfriend. Marriage? The holy grail.

But can I be a total downer and point out that half of marriages end in divorce? If you were having a surgery that had a fifty-fifty success rate, you'd be like, "No fucking way." But for some reason with marriage, we're like, "Eh, I'll take the risk."

As a result, instead of focusing on our self-development, we date to marry, and then when we get there, a lot of us are trapped in a legal union we might have to pay thousands of dollars to escape (and take on approximately twenty-seven tons of guilt over wedding gifts we will absolutely keep even though the marriage went to shit). We are fed this falsehood of marriage being the end goal of dating, but when we achieve it, no one is there to give us our prize. In terms of life experi-ences that bring joy and exhilaration, nobody puts marriage on their bucket list as something you HAVE to experience before you die. It's a beautiful, life-affirming thing when it works. But when it doesn't, no one looks back on their life and says happily, "I was fucking miserable, but I was mar-ried!"

I don't know what my life will look like when this book comes out, but I do know that any relationship I find myself in going forward, I enter with a solid foundation and sense of self because of the time I've spent alone.

As corny as it sounds, I don't think I really grew as a person—mentally, spiritually, even health-wise—until I learned how to be my own friend. And it didn't happen through anything complex, like a silent retreat where I did trust falls with myself into a contemplation pool, or took ayahuasca and talked to my inner child.

The simplest way to foster a good relationship with yourself is to ask yourself how you treat your friends. You probably listen to them, compliment them, encourage them, and set them straight when they're being too hard on themselves. You don't allow them to accept things that aren't good enough for them. You don't let them get stuck in unhealthy situations. Okay! Now, just apply that to the way you treat yourself. Show yourself the same respect and care because no one can do this for you—it starts and ends with you.

Once you've adopted the mindset, time to put things into action. And again, it's not that hard. It just starts with spending time solo. It's really that simple. *You can't know yourself unless you spend quality time alone.* Emphasis on quality. We've talked about enjoying being single, but this goes deeper—it's not just spending time with yourself because you're not in a relationship. (In fact, if you are in a relationship, solitary time is even more important.) This is about carving out time for self-exploration and space in your schedule that is solely focused on delving into your interests and what makes you happy.

I'm at my happiest when I'm alone in my house writing (or let's face it, making TikToks and Instagram stories). I've always been that way, long before I made a career out of satirizing Rich Moms and posting pics of seafood platters. I used to retreat to my room as a kid and make stuff for hours on end. These days when I've had too much on the calendar, too many weeks in a row, I start to feel this creeping feeling that I'm losing touch with myself. It definitely shows in what I put out in the world too—the less alone time I get, the shittier my content gets. But when I block out a week to recharge (what I call "plug in the wall" time), suddenly I get the spark back. I know I can't be my best self if I don't collect my thoughts and vibe alone.

In this section, we'll be talking a lot about self-work and less about how to navigate dating. And my hope is that by the end of the section, you'll understand why.

THE SHIFT: When will I meet someone? → How do I make sure I know myself when I eventually do?

GOOD IDEAS FROM BAD PLACES:
PULLING CREATIVITY OUT OF CHAOS

"In the midst of the darkness, grab a flashlight."

—Gabrielle Bernstein, *The Universe Has Your Back*

As a wise and probably boring man once said, everything in moderation. There's a fine line to walk when it comes to spending time alone, and I've learned the hard way that when I *realllly* isolate myself I can start to go off the deep end. When it's a pandemic and I have no choice but to isolate myself every day for weeks as an unemployed person living in a new city? Let's just say I went off the deep end with a cinder block tied to my ankle.

During the early days of 2020 quarantine, I would get up and just walk around LA for hours every day. I literally had nothing else to do. I didn't even have a couch in my apartment. I watched TV on my laptop and scrolled desperately through articles and websites, grasping for straws and anything I could cling to that would give me a momentary break from my own thoughts. I was wildly depressed and felt like a complete failure. I thought, okay, I gave Los Angeles my all, but I need to call it. I planned to move back home to London as soon as possible. It actually felt like an A or B choice: Either move home or die.

Of course, I couldn't actually go anywhere for a while, so I had to make a survival plan in the meantime. I don't know how or why this particular method came to me, but I decided that in order to get through this period, I would pretend I was a teenager again. Like I was locked in the house, grounded. But I could do anything I wanted within the confines of my own room. I would stay up late, eat junk food, sleep till noon.

And that's exactly what I did. I ate chicken fingers and ordered silly lights for my bedroom. (Do you guys remember the TikTok lights that made your ceiling look like the night sky? The ones meant for teenagers? Yeah. I got those.) I threw myself into my crush list and would obsessively daydream about guys I'd never met or dudes I had been friends with for years (which led to fucking my Friend, see page 162). Slowly but surely, I slipped into a state of mind I hadn't been in for almost a decade.

A few weeks into the experiment, I realized that a huge part of my teenage years was having the freedom to be creative—because I was so unwell. Throughout high school, I had such crippling anxiety and borderline OCD that I would seclude myself up in my room and make stuff, completely detached from the outcome. I was just moved to create. I would make sculptures and collages, research Pedro Almodóvar and stay up until four in the morning watching all of his films, or fanatically read every book Chuck Palahniuk had ever written. I had no preconceived notions, no fear of judgment. (And lots of undiagnosed ADHD!)

Now as an adult or something like it, who had tapped into a juvenile freedom that could only be summoned by extreme mental instability, my creative juices went into writing and making TikToks. It took some getting used to, especially as a former freelance writer who thought in terms of price per word. I had to make a Herculean effort to quiet that voice in my head that whispered, "Tinx, you're not even getting paid for this." Besides, I wasn't making any money anyway! So I let myself write for the sake of writing and create for the sake of creating.

I started slowly, just observing what was already on Tik-Tok, which was mostly dancing at the time. But there were also these short videos that I can only describe as live-action memes—you know, an audio clip that people would take and add their own video and caption to. For some reason, my brain just immediately understood the format—it reminded me of (stay with me here) Shakespearean sonnets, where you took a preestablished form and added your own meaning to it. Just me? In any case, I realized that it made me happy and gave me a spark I hadn't felt in a very long time. I have to admit, it's pretty funny that in the midst of my late-twenties teenage regression, I stumbled into TikTok like Steve Buscemi holding a skateboard and saying, "How do you do, fellow kids?" But you know what? It was exactly what I needed—community, creativity, and zero barrier to entry.

I don't recommend my entire quarantine regimen, but I will say that tapping back into an adolescent mindset can really unlock your imagination. When we're teenagers, we can feel inspired by just about anything. But as we get older, we see everything on a work-play binary, where play feels irresponsible or a waste of time. We rarely just do things for the hell of it. Everything has to be for a purpose. For every endeavor we ask ourselves, "How is this going to help me?" Ironically, this zaps us of our passion and disconnects us from that fourteen-year-old who came up with wild, original ideas and allowed themselves to just go with it. That's why my number one piece of advice for people going through a tough time isn't "self-care." I suggest you take on a silly little project. Maybe it's creating a gallery wall in your hallway. Maybe it's refreshing your Spotify playlists. Let yourself get completely immersed in it and you'll reunite with that kid who wasted hours upon hours in her room, creating magic.

> **THE SHIFT:** What am I working toward? → What's a project I can do just for fun?

This is something I've had to remind myself especially while writing this book. It's really hard for me to stay in the present. I'm always thinking, "When this happens, then I'll do that . . ." I'm obsessed with checkpoints and working toward a goal. But I've been trying to fall more in love with the process, because that's the beautiful part. And that's why my depressive periods can be so fruitful, because I give up on working toward anything at all. Everything else falls to the wayside. I say no to social obligations. I wear the same pair of sweatpants for a week. It's all stripped away, and I'm just left with my wild, naked thoughts.

I find immense periods of growth come out of these periods of darkness and there have been three times this has been particularly true: high school, quarantine, and the time my old tweets resurfaced. Excuse me while I take a shot before we get into the next chapter.

HOW TO LOSE FRIENDS AND INFLUENCE PEOPLE

"That which hurts, also instructs."

—Benjamin Franklin

My job is weird. If you had asked me as a girl what I wanted to be when I grew up, I might have said "actress" but I certainly wouldn't have said "influencer." Mostly because it didn't exist at the time, and also because I've never wanted to be famous. I landed in this career more as a result of being a people pleaser with a touch of narcissist who gets off on making people laugh. When the barrier to entry became "Can you operate a phone and think in terms of memes?" I realized I had a future in the biz.

However, what's kept me in this career are the followers who, not to be dramatic, are the reason I get up in the morning. More than anything, I do this job because I want people to have a space where they can take a break and feel seen. I simply want to share what I've learned and distill some collective wisdom that women can pull from in difficult or confusing times throughout their lives. Since getting a sizable following, I also do my best not to share negative views about anyone because I'd rather put positive content into the world. My professional motto has been "Work Hard and Be Nice to People."

So it's been fascinating, and terrifying, to get a glimpse into the inner workings of the influencer industry. It's important to discuss, because it's not just an issue that affects people with blue checks next to their name—it says something about our society and the way we invest in, create false intimacy with, and idolize the people on our screens . . . and how we love to watch them burn.

The word "Schadenfreude" means to take pleasure in another person's misfortune. The Germans coined the term in the nineteenth century, when it probably referred to being secretly delighted that your neighbor's mustard crop had a poor harvest because they had been obnoxiously flaunting their new horse and buggy to everyone in town. They couldn't possibly have known the levels we'd take it to with social media, where you can watch the rise and fall of a real person's life as if it were a dark comedy made solely for your entertainment. We gobble up news about a seemingly perfect Hollywood couple's breakup, a successful celebrity's DUI, and an influencer's fall from grace. Is it just a human instinct to crane your neck and look at the accident as you drive by? Or is it an evil, unnatural impulse that we've allowed to thrive in the last twentyish years? I never asked myself these questions before I became internet famous. I never looked at a star's fuckup and thought, "There but for the grace of God go I." Until I climbed right into the belly of the beast and experienced it for myself.

I often refer to the changes that people go through when they get famous as "going through the purple machine." Picture, if you will, a big purple machine, and you're on some sort of conveyor belt. As you enter the purple machine, your hair, face, and body get transformed from normal-person status to shiny, perfect, stylized celeb. No more doing your own hair and makeup, now you have a glam squad. You couldn't possibly pick out your own clothes anymore, you have a stylist going forward. Even your social media gets a gloss treatment, with a sudden disappearance of candid lip-syncs in the car, thrown out in favor of #sponcon, brand events, and unboxings.

Suddenly the people who were rooting for you as one of their favorite accounts to follow are rolling their eyes at how much you've changed. You start to get trolled. On the outside, you're blowing up. But on the inside, the energy has shifted. With every thousand new followers, you somehow feel more and more alone. You have more brand deals than you know what to do with, but every time you post the branded content that is now paying your rent, you get complaints and demands to "bring back the old you."

You used to be described as "relatable," but now the only way in which you're described is in relation to how many followers you have. As strange and gross as it feels, though, it's oddly addictive. You're drunk on the validation. And this is when the purple machine that made you does you dirty, because on your "rise to fame" you never bothered to check to see where the conveyor belt was going. It carried you up and up until you were too high to see over the crest. And that's exactly when the machine drops you.

In the spring of 2022, there was an article written with the title "We Need to Talk About Tinx's Old Tweets." The writer had collected about ten tweets from between 2012 and 2020 that included some truly abhorrent comments I'd made about celebrities, political issues, and COVID. Most were not my original tweets but things I'd casually—okay, let's be honest, mindlessly—liked or retweeted (many while in the depths of a head-spinning depression and the first few weeks of a terrifying pandemic).

The mean tweets were beyond embarrassing and unearthed some major issues I'd been struggling with in my twenties (don't worry, we'll go there soon). And the ones from 2020? Well, I'd been living like a fourteen-year-old, with no regard for the future, clinging to anything that would distract me from the loss of control I felt. It was a strange time, and I coped by doom scrolling, not realizing I was engaging with hurtful, harmful, and flat-out fake news content. I deserve to be taken to task for that. Adding to misinformation, xenophobic thought, or divisive rhetoric is inexcusable, and I will always be ashamed of what I did.

At the time, I had zero following. No responsibility to "use my platform" because I had no platform to speak of, with the exception of perhaps twenty-seven random followers. I certainly didn't think I was actually endorsing anything. I wasn't thinking, period. I was alone, lonely, hitting my late twenties in a new city. I was trying to find my voice, and I thought I had to punch low or be outrageous to stand out. Of course, I just ended up acting out like an asshole. If it were most people, it would have gone into the ether of regrettable decisions. But suddenly, it looked like this would be etched on my tombstone.

What was striking was the glee with which the old-tweet controversy was met. People seemed to be having so much fun seeing me fall from grace. There was a sense of catharsis and revelry around it, without anyone digging deeper. No one took a step back and said, "Actually, her progressive tweets outnumber any conservative-leaning ones ninety-nine to one." Because that's not a good headline, it's too nuanced, and at the end of the day, it was less about what my actual political beliefs were and more about nailing me and watching me go down in flames.

What felt even worse was knowing that the followers who had supported me so consistently were disappointed in me, and the audience I'd worked so hard to build misunderstood who I really was. That handful of old tweets did not represent me or my true opinions, and yet it seemed to undo all the other content I'd put into the world. It broke my heart that the women I'd given dating advice, and reminders to prioritize themselves and take care of their friends, would now have any ounce of confusion around the kind of person I really was.

There was a moment when I considered just deleting my Twitter. But as I sat with it, I realized that getting rid of my tweets just seemed fake. People had started following me because I was a real person. And I'd been very open about missteps I'd made in the past, including some very nasty posts. I decided to leave it as it was, warts and all, instead of scrubbing my account the first moment I got a glimpse of success (and criticism).

Meanwhile, the hate became so intense, I felt almost catatonic in response. Reddit went wild. My entire feed was filled with people posting "Why I'm Unfollowing Tinx" and "Why Tinx Is Toxic" videos. Press was coming out with dramatic headlines and zero context. People were posting my home address and saying they were going to kill me and my cat.

Was I the victim here? No, I deserved to take accountability for my mistakes. But did the punishment fit the crime? If you think that because I liked a tweet I should get death threats, you have a pretty weird idea of justice.

I had woken up every day for two years and created content for free, spent hours giving advice in my DMs, trying to boost other people up. Of course, I had also gotten so much in return—professionally and personally. The gratitude I felt around what I got to do for a living and all the benefits that came with it had motivated me every day to give more to my followers. I guess I just thought that all of that would have meant something. I thought actions spoke louder than retweets.

Like all great thought leaders, I took to Instagram to issue an apology. Meanwhile, the bad news kept coming in. This brand partnership dropped. That photo shoot canceled. Zero emails in the inbox.

The first time I did my live call-in radio show in the midst of all of this, I was terrified that every call would be someone screaming at me. I couldn't drink or take a Xanax to calm my nerves before the show because it was eight in the morning and I really needed to be on. But . . . I definitely thought about it. I threw up in the studio bathroom and then somehow got it together.

We had like five hundred calls and not one of the trolls showed up. No one had the nerve to say any of the things they said in the comments to my face (or at least to my voice on the other end of the line). The people who did call in brought me back to reality. They asked about long-distance relationships, about how to handle ghosting, and how to carve out time for yourself when you're coupled up. I felt more clarity than I had in weeks. I'd honestly been thinking of quitting the whole business altogether. But then I realized it would mean giving up on helping people. It would mean throwing away the only thing I'd found that gave my life real purpose.

Before this whole episode, I was doing everything for brand deals and invites. I couldn't say no to anything. But when all of that was nearly taken away, it forced me to look at myself and see that I was really struggling. I was working so hard but had no sense of what it was all worth. It made me realize that fame and money and the excitement of being in the spotlight were certainly great in their own ways, but when I was faced with them being stripped away, it also felt freeing. I was like, all right, I don't have to do any brand deals this week. No parties I have to go to. It emphasized what was really important to me, what I actually like to do, whom I like to spend time with, and what I actually want to say.

And with that realization I discovered that I hadn't been using my own voice in a long time. I was coasting. I didn't have a point of view. I would call my therapist sobbing when everything was good because I felt beholden to all these people who didn't give a fuck about me. I tripped out on getting people into parties and being seen. Losing all the fringe benefits and responsibilities that came with influencer fame brought me back to the reason I got into this in the first place: to express myself and share my honest experiences and opinions. Going forward, I just don't want to lose my spark again. I want to be real, not just by showing my stretch marks and hip dips, but by being genuinely flawed and using my platform to (responsibly) highlight the things that bring me joy and talk about the things I might be struggling with.

It's complicated, though. As an influencer, it's my job to

share what I love. But people confuse it and think I'm trying to write a universal prescription to everyone on the planet. *Opinion is not instruction!* I once said I hated *Schitt's Creek* and instead of people responding, "I disagree with you because of the humor of Moira . . ." it was "You're wrong. You're evil." It's silly that I have to preface almost everything I say with "This is just my opinion," because . . . obviously it is?

I know that if people didn't put weight on what I say, I wouldn't have the life that I do. But perhaps our reliance on online strangers can be a little misplaced sometimes. It used to be that you would go to your neighbor and say, "My kid's got a rash, what should I do?" But now we look to people we have no real connection to, like we can replace our actual community and real leaders. And we develop these one-sided parasocial relationships with influencers, so when something doesn't completely align with our ideals, it feels like an all-out attack on a bond we've created in our minds.

I love coming across something that changes my mind. It's why I read all the time. For example, I've always been very cut-and-dry about cheating—no room for gray area. But I read *Tiny Beautiful Things* by Cheryl Strayed, and there's this essay about cheating that really made me see it in a new light. I'm never going to condone cheating, but I realized there can be a lot of nuance.

Same thing with marriage. In my younger years, I was adamant that I would never marry. And then I started reading a lot of female memoirs by people such as Diane von Furstenberg and Demi Moore, and they talked about it in a way that opened my mind and made me want to (maybe?) try it one day.

> **THE SHIFT:** There's clearly a right answer, and it's mine →
> Strong opinions loosely held

So, I went through the purple box and I almost lost myself. But along came another conveyor belt that swept me into a big silver car wash contraption that pelted me, sprayed me, and humbled me. It stripped everything away, leaving me with nothing but gratitude, renewed purpose, and stringy wet hair. To be honest, I will never be the same—the experience has truly fucked with me and I don't think I will ever get over the things that were said. I had spent thirty-one years figuring out who I was (which is someone layered and flawed but also giving and loving) and it rocked me to see my entire personhood reduced to clickbait headlines. But the silver (car wash) lining is that it forced me to work harder to define who I am. And the way that shows up in my everyday life is by having opinions, and being unashamed to share them, while being open enough to call bullshit on myself.

What does this have to do with anything and why is this in a relationship book? Well, if you don't form some strong opinions—*and* have to defend them from time to time—then you are more susceptible to losing yourself when you get into a relationship down the line. It absolutely doesn't mean you have to be with someone who agrees with you on every issue. But you have to know where they stand and what really matters to you. *Remaining neutral in order to be likable is a trap because eventually you discover that without any opinions, you don't know who you are.* By forming opinions, and by making priorities, you discover who you truly are.

HOES OVER BROS:

HOW TO BE A BETTER FRIEND

> "Bitch, you look goodt, with a T at the end / I'ma hype
> her every time, that my motherfuckin' friend."
>
> **—Saweetie, "Best Friend"**

I will never forget the friends who were there for me during the darkest-time-of-my-life episode: Daisy, Dena, Ashley, Chloe, Lucas, Seth, Saba, Lauren, Camilla, Greg, John . . . I'm listing these people by name because I truly might not have made it through without them. (Two more shout-outs who aren't technically "friends": my mom, who deserves a medal for staying on the phone with me for hours while I cried, and my therapist, who is probably still recovering from the demands I placed on her.)

For a few weeks, I didn't leave my house. I wasn't sleeping. I wasn't eating. My friends just took turns coming to sit with me. To be honest, I don't remember anything that my friends said during this time. I remember them calling me to say they were coming over. I remember them showing up with food. I remember them texting each morning to make sure that I was okay. Nobody offered up anything earth-shattering that changed my mind about the situation—at least not that I can remember. They simply sat with me through it. And I will never, ever forget that.

I fell more deeply in love with my friends than I thought possible—the ones who showed me they were the real ones. It's when I had an epiphany about the real meaning of friendship. I'd always equated a big part of friendship with fun. (And if I'm being honest, partying.) But this completely redefined my old beliefs. *It's easy to be someone's friend when everything's easy.* It's fun to be someone's friend when they are inviting you to parties or giving you free stuff. But to be with someone when they have nothing to give you and when they are so, so low is a different level of friendship and compassion. What my friends did for me during that time taught me a lot about just showing up. Nothing else really matters.

I get a lot of questions about how to help a friend going through a tough situation, and I would urge you not to over-think it or get too hung up on saying the right thing. The "what should I say?" anxiety is simply our ego getting in the way. All you need to do is send a text saying, "I'm coming over." Or "You don't have to respond, but I'm thinking about you." *You don't have to take away the discomfort—all you have to do is make sure your friend doesn't sit in it alone.* That shit goes a long way.

> **THE SHIFT:** I don't know what to say ⟶ Just show up

I've already written about the special role that male friend-ships have played in my life, but female friendships are really the thing I hold more sacred than anything in the universe. It started when I was a little girl, growing up between two countries, feeling out of place in both, and spending most of my time with adults. It was a little bizarre and a lot lonely. I always longed for a sister (no offense to my little brother). Luckily, going to an all-girls school was like getting a bunch of built-in sisters. I loved the camaraderie. I loved the uniform. From a very early age, I understood the importance of female solidarity. Even though the school was extremely competitive and somewhat cliquey, it was also a safe place where there was a shared understanding—no need to act differently around the boys, no need to feel shame as a young girl getting boobs and starting your period, and complete freedom to focus on the things that mattered: good grades and getting a part in the school play.

Thus, I am a girl's girl, through and through. But not all of us are steered so clearly down this lane. Scarcity mindset gets indoctrinated at such a young age that even in elementary school there's often an automatic assessment among girls, sizing each other up to see who's prettier or smarter instead of opening our arms and boosting each other up. Then social media takes that competitive mindset and turns the volume all the way up. We forget the power and potential we hold when we band together because it's just too easy to feel like we're all in some kind of contest. (Unless, of course, you find yourself drunk in a women's restroom with a girl you've known for thirty seconds, in which case the brainwashing gets canceled out, you can only gush over how gorgeous her lipstick is, and you will give her the shirt off your back.)

If you weren't born with the gal-pal gene, can you teach yourself to become more of a girl's girl? I think you can and the key is being vulnerable. You have to actively reject all sense of competition and replace it with honesty. Not just in that quirky "I spilled an entire coffee on myself this morning!" way, but in doing things like telling your new coworker that you're terrified of giving presentations because you feel unqualified, or initiating a conversation with that girl in your workout class who you just think seems really cool—and telling her just that.

And instead of doing a side-by-side analysis when you meet another girl, think about what the two of you share. Being a woman is such a unique and complex experience and I love bonding over the nuances with fellow females. Think of each one you meet as a comrade who has struggled with many of the same things you've struggled with. *If only we allowed ourselves to rely on each other more, if we opened up about what we secretly worried about, if every time we brought a group of women together we could crowdsource all of the collective wisdom, we could save ourselves so much time.* So let's try to help each other figure out the answers and have each other's backs, shall we?

Obviously that applies to making new friends, but just as important is nurturing the friendships you already have. This could probably warrant an entire book unto itself, so I will do my best to coalesce the main points here. Most important, especially as we get older, is acknowledging that friendships ebb and flow and that there will be periods of intense closeness and periods where life and circumstances get in the way. This isn't a reflection on your bond (unless it is, and you just don't have any connection anymore, which does happen). But if you're in your thirties and have a few friends you've been tight with since high school or college, it's safe to say those are your lifers, and while you need to stoke the friendship flames every once in a while, a few weeks or even months won't mean the end of your relationship forever.

On a practical level, I would advise you to not put a ton of pressure on speaking frequently. Let's face it, scheduling catch-up sessions or playing phone tag is a goddamn nightmare. You probably don't know your friend's day-to-day schedule as well as you used to and that's okay. What's more approachable and far less daunting is an occasional text. And for the love of God, none of these "Miss youuuuu, it's been forever! How are you??" That's too broad. Instead, send them a little glimpse into your life ("Omg I'm about to go on a Tinder date with a guy and I'm feeling bajiggity! Talk me off the ledge") or bring up a random memory ("Remember that chihuahua in San Luis Obispo with the huge balls? Just thinking of him, and you. Love you!") and don't feel like you have to give these long, formal state-of-affairs updates, even if it's been a while since you guys chatted.

> **THE SHIFT:** I'm scared our friendship is going to change ⟶
> It's going to anyway, so take the pressure off

Last but not least, let's discuss Fatal Flaw Theory. This originated with an old friend of mine who was a chronic one-upper. It drove me up the wall because I couldn't understand why she felt the need to turn everything into a competition, especially when we were such close friends. I was complaining about it to my mom, and she kindly but firmly told me, "Honey, she's your friend. That's part of her personality. And you're either going to need to accept that, or stop being friends with her." Was I gobsmacked! My mom had a point. The energy I was wasting harping on a trait that I knew she'd always had (and probably would always have) was only harming me, and tarnishing what was otherwise a beautiful friendship. So I accepted it, and suddenly her attempts to top whatever I said or did stopped bothering me.

Which brings us to the Fatal Flaw Theory. We all have one. Mine is impatience. One of my friend's is moodiness. Yours might be that you're always late. Your friend might be kinda cheap. Whatever it is, you need to acknowledge it, and either accept it as part of their personality (or at least let it become something you can learn to expect so it doesn't ruffle your feathers so much) or use it to reevaluate the relationship if it's something that is truly harmful or disrespectful.

The main thing to remember is that just because someone has a fatal flaw doesn't mean they can't be a good friend. When you can accept slightly annoying traits that are simply part of someone's personality, you reinforce the importance of that friendship and that the positives outweigh any negatives. On the other hand, if someone's fatal flaw has a direct impact on your happiness or self-esteem, it may be time to focus on other friendships that build you up.

> **THE SHIFT:** There she goes again (eye roll) → There she goes again (classic Stacy!)

Speaking of negative Nancies, I want to make an important distinction. You can and should help a friend going through a tough time. But if the negativity is more of an everyday, rain-or-shine thing, or the relationship is more of a "take take take" dynamic, it's okay to step away. Especially if the negativity is directed toward you in a competitive or critical way. Or if a large part of the conversation with them revolves around talking shit about other people. Sometimes it can be disguised as a "tell it like it is" or "no bullshit" friend, but there's a difference between keeping it real and cutting other people down. A friend only builds you up—anything else is just a strong clue that they fear your greatest potential.

I basically take on the vibe of every person, child, pet, or city I come in contact with, so this boundary has been especially crucial for my well-being. Especially in LA. It took me a while to recognize that the Bay Area me was completely different from the New York me and the LA me. When I first got to LA, I hung out with some mean people because they seemed cool and I was wrapped up in the idea of being in the right crowd. But it was no coincidence that my early days in LA coincided with a deep depression and lack of joy. You are the sum of the people you spend the most time with. Your vibe attracts your tribe, as the mug from Target says.

It may seem extreme, but I honestly believe that energy is infectious and subtly toxic people inflict just as much damage as openly violent or aggressive people. It's an IV drip that slowly kills you rather than a whack in the back of the head. So you have to protect yourself. *If someone was threatening your physical safety you probably wouldn't hang out with them, right? The same should apply to your energy.*

> **THE SHIFT:** Your friends are your friends no matter what —→
> What kind of energy do I want to curate in my relationships?

The bottom line is that your friends are a reflection of how you see yourself. This applies to dating as well, because a woman with a really tight, supportive friend group will be much less likely to put up with bullshit from a man who doesn't deserve her. Her girls have her back and that radiates outward in the way she expects to be treated by a partner. Conversely, if you surround yourself with friends who don't constantly remind you how absolutely incredible you are, you're more likely to seek validation from a man—and that's setting yourself up for an unequal relationship from the jump.

What about when the call is coming from inside the house? If you are your worst critic (and your friends and family constantly tell you not to be so hard on yourself), then go back to that idea of being a friend to yourself, and don't say anything to yourself that you wouldn't say to your best friend. Even better, lean on a girlfriend and let her hype you up.

IF YOU DON'T HAVE ANYTHING NICE TO SAY:

A BETTER WAY TO TALK ABOUT BODIES

"Hurt people hurt people."

—Unknown

I've always been told I was funny. I've always looked up to people who are funny. I've always considered "You have a way with words" to be one of the highest compliments one can receive. I spent my twenties trying to figure out how to channel that ambiguous drive and desire into something that resembled a career.

I tried on a lot of hats. I thought I wanted to work in fashion so I got jobs at Gap Inc. and Poshmark. I started freelance writing for *Teen Vogue* and PopSugar. I went to Parsons to get my master's in fashion journalism. I dreamed of living in New York and working in magazines. As I attempted to become the next Carrie Bradshaw–meets–Andie Anderson, I looked at what else was out there and what kind of online articles were getting attention. We weren't too far out from the height of the Perez Hilton days, when he brutally roasted celebrities for their addictions, outfits, weight gain, or mental instability. We were still living in a time when being fat was a punch line (*Shallow Hal*, Monica from *Friends*, Chris from *Just Friends*, I could go on), where getting a reaction out of people meant being grating and mean. I thought maybe I could be like a young Joan Rivers (with no following whatsoever). So I said Tori Spelling was ugly. And I called my queen and savior Kim Kardashian fat.

Here's the truth: I was never fat-phobic. I was a miserable person who hated herself. Keep in mind I had approximately seventeen followers, so these posts felt more like yelling into a void than making an actual statement that other people would read—never mind the celebrities I was making fun of. I was hung up on my own outward appearance and projected that insecurity onto others as a way to make myself feel better. Like I was somehow superior if I could point the finger elsewhere instead of dealing with the crippling preoccupation I had with my own body. It was lazy, it was immature, and it was such shitty content.

Here's what I should have been posting about: Up until my late twenties, the most important thing to me was striving for some sort of physical standard that I could never meet. I was obsessed with being thin. In college, I abused Adderall (to control my ADHD and curb my appetite—a multitasking girl's best friend) and flirted with different eating disorders. (Part of me resisted writing this part, because what woman hasn't dealt with disordered eating? Isn't it a terrible rite of passage for all young girls growing up in the patriarchy?) I would get wasted and force myself to throw up my dinner. Thankfully, my boyfriend caught on and told me I had to stop or he'd break up with me. So of course, I stopped. Not for myself, but so I wouldn't lose him.

I tried every single diet, switching from one to the next with no break in between. The more outlandish a diet sounded, the more it seemed like it might hold the secret to finally achieving the body I dreamed of. Before a trip to Miami with my best friend, Dena, I tried the Dukan Diet. If you haven't heard of it, it's the one where you just eat meat for three days straight and then you go into ketosis. My boyfriend at the time, Arthur, could smell the meat fumes coming off me.

On the trip, I remember the distinct rush of feeling super thin. I posted my first bikini pic on Instagram, because the whole point of achieving the body I wanted was to offer it up for public consumption. I thought I was being sexually empowered, but despite having had lots of sex by this point, I hadn't come into my sexuality yet, it was all about the performance and the external validation. My body wasn't mine at all.

When I look back at photos from that trip, they show a seemingly happy person. What the photos don't show is that I was basically dead inside. I was so hung up on what I looked like that I sacrificed how I felt. The diet included such unpleasant side effects as rotten breath, constipation, and overall feelings of wanting to barf and sleep all day. In other words, it was a bit unsustainable. So after that trip I kept trying other methods, all of them with varying levels of miserable results. I can't tell you how much time and effort I wasted on all of these fruitless experiments. And let me tell you what I had to learn the hard way: The reason there are so many different diets is because none of them work.

If only I had pursued my professional ambitions and creative aspirations as diligently as I pursued my weight goals. As a twentysomething with no other accomplishments to speak of at the time, having a thin body was my only status symbol. Unfortunately, it got worse before it got better.

When I moved to New York, I hired an insane nutritionist who worked with all the models—it was rumored he had helped Bella and Gigi Hadid. Thus began the most restrictive time of my life. The program involved eating no fruit whatsoever, ingesting (that's the only word that feels appropriate) weird bars and shakes in the morning, and staying away from anything else that wasn't a vegetable. There was a weigh-in every two weeks that felt about as high stakes as an episode of *Squid Game*. My weight went up and down like crazy and when I told the nutritionist guy I wanted to be 130 pounds he said, "Well, you aren't living a hundred-and-thirty-pound lifestyle." Despite the fact I was starving myself.

It would have been bad enough if that was the extent of it, but the fucked-up scrutiny toward myself radiated outward toward other people as well. I realize now that the times when I felt worse about myself were also when I would be more mean. Because I felt out of control, judging other women became a way to prove to myself that they couldn't control their lives either.

Truly, it wasn't until I found TikTok and my audience that I came to a healthy place with my body. I talked honestly about the bullying comments I'd made in the past and how I'd been mean. But it didn't really click for me until that audience with whom I'd come to have one of the most important relationships in my life was in jeopardy. I had to really examine the nature of my body negativity. Now I try to be the influencer I needed when I was in my twenties. Someone who advocates that enjoying margaritas, chips, and guac with your friends is so much more important than what size jeans you wear. Yes, I still do cleanses once or twice a year, but I need a reset every once in a while because I fucking love to eat and drink with abandon and unfortunately I'm the kind of person who needs to block out five days in her calendar to actually just stay home and not go out every night.

I've just gotten to a point where I embrace the duality of doing whatever I want to do and knowing when I need to reign it in in order to take better care of myself. If not restricting myself anymore means my body looks a little different, I don't care. I mean, I don't really care. Okay, I care a lot less. Gaining five pounds used to fucking destroy me. And now it just bothers me a little.

I'm saying all of this because I think it's so fucked up to add to the pressure we put on women by telling them not to care so much about their weight. I grew up in the nineties and early aughts, when Kate Moss was on the cover of every magazine, JLo was basically the curviest woman they allowed in Hollywood, and Bridget Jones labeled 134 pounds as fat. Excuse me for holding myself to unrealistic standards. I was born into it! It's easier for younger people who grew up with the privilege of seeing different body types represented in the mainstream to criticize any content that comes across as anything but all-embracing. But that is ignoring an important reality of what women my age and older grew up with. It's reductive and dismissive of a huge part of our psyche. Saying "weight is just a number" means that if you care about it—because you've been culturally conditioned to—there's something wrong with you. Somehow we've gone from shaming women for having cellulite to shaming them if they feel ashamed about it. I think it's more compassionate to acknowledge how much we think about it and to acknowledge what a struggle it can be.

> **THE SHIFT:** Love your body no matter what! ⟶ Appreciate what your body can do for you

This book is all about shifting your perspective, and this might be one of the most impactful shifts you can make: to recognize the power that negative body image has over you, and then go one step further to understand that that feeling does not serve you. It does not help you in any way.

So many women contact me after fun, indulgent vacations they've taken, or after a particularly hard time in which their bodies have changed, and say they feel disgusted with themselves. If you're ever in that position, I urge you to take a step back and ask, "Would I ever feel disgusted with my friend or sister if she gained weight?" Tell yourself what you'd tell a friend if you caught them bashing themselves.

And keep telling yourself. This isn't a shift that happens once and lasts forever. Because of the wonderfully fucked-up society we live in, it's often daily progress you have to maintain. But instead of the calorie-counting, hormone-destroying, and all-consuming business of being on a diet, you'll be able to do something other than think about food and your body. Your life will open up to so many greater things.

Take it from me: Once you give yourself back the time wasted on pursuing physical perfection (which doesn't exist! and can't ever be achieved through berating yourself!), it leads to all the things that actually make you feel confident: Better sex. Better guys. Better everything.

BEST HOUR OF THE WEEK:

WHAT THERAPY HAS TAUGHT ME

"Therapy is like dating—there's no one-size-fits-all."

—Tinx Original

The first time I went to therapy I was about thirteen. My best friend moved away, and I had a bit of a breakdown. I hadn't been sleeping because I was terrified that someone would kidnap me in the middle of the night. I'd learn about a random disease and get so paranoid that I'd have to research all the information I could find about it. I'd read the Wikipedia synopsis of every horror movie because I figured if I knew how they all ended, I'd be prepared for every single situation. Luckily my parents encouraged me to be open about what I was struggling with and did everything they could to get me the help I needed.

I didn't love the first therapist I went to, but I immediately loved the experience of therapy. The idea of investigating my neuroses and trying to become a better version of myself has always been exciting to me. I eventually found a therapist I vibed with and began regular talk therapy, where I realized that the most important thing I could do for myself was just to not hold all these worries hostage in my head. I was able to identify and label my thoughts and my trusty lifelong companions, Mr. Anxiety and Mr. Depression.

In college, things got better, but unfortunately Mr. Anxiety had gotten a full ride to attend with me. I would randomly call my mom crying, asking, "Do you think I have cancer?" There was a lot of running downstairs to touch the door three times, checking under the bed three times—you know, super-cool normal sorority-girl stuff. But I was busy and loved school and my friends. For the most part, I was genuinely happy. My therapy kind of lapsed and it felt like finally I had my shit together.

Then I moved to New York for grad school, not realizing that Mr. Depression had decided to stow away in my suitcase. Pretty much upon arrival, I realized I'd made a terrible mistake. I felt alone, scared, and very lost, especially as all my friends' lives started to take shape and left me looking at my own like a failure. I found a new therapist and met my therapy soulmate, cognitive behavioral therapy. CBT is practical, actionable, and results-driven. She is me. Together, we got out of that dark place, and I began to see a light at the end of the tunnel. I made the decision to move back to LA because California is my spiritual home and I thought it would be best for my mental health to never wear a floor-length down parka ever again. It was one hundred percent the right move, but as I'm a creature of habit and routine, even good changes are hard for me. With the pandemic sprinkled in, Mr. Depression decided to leave New York, move across the country, and be my roommate in LA, picking up Mr. Anxiety along the way. Three's company too!

I went back to therapy, started taking medication that helped, and found a new career that finally gave me a sense of purpose. However, as my following grew, along came the trolls. I started getting panic attacks from the comments they left. There were times I thought I should go to the hospital because Mr. Anxiety had me cornered, stomping on my chest so I couldn't breathe.

I had finally gotten to a personal and professional place I'd never imagined was possible, and people I didn't know (and who didn't know jack shit about me) threatened to take it all away. The stakes were too high to allow this to keep me from my goals, so I doubled down with my therapist and we came up with a plan to set boundaries around how I would handle the weird world of internet fame. I now have a toolkit I can reach for anytime the haters rear their heads, which is—bless their souls—just about every day.

One of the main tools my therapist has armed me with is the idea of "low mood." I have a tendency to quickly spiral and catastrophize when things go wrong, making a less-than-ideal situation into something that seems life-threatening. And when I'm feeling stressed, no one can talk me out of it or make me feel better by saying, "Everything is going to be fine." That enrages me. But what does actually help is saying, "Okay, sounds like you're in a low mood. That's why everything feels more intense." Labeling it really makes a difference. And identifying all the stress as simply a side effect of a dip in the atmosphere is comforting because a low mood—or any mood really—is never permanent.

Honestly, nothing is permanent. Not to be all monk about it, but the number one thing that my therapist has taught me is just how to stay present and the immense effect that has on your well-being. As a professional future tripper and president of the Reverse Box Fan Club, I'm constantly thinking about the next thing, while ignoring the thing right in front of me that I've dreamed of and worked toward for years. Therapy has helped me to stop and smell the fake roses (I can't keep plants alive and another huge milestone in my journey was just accepting that).

Even when things are going relatively smoothly, I still need therapy. In fact, those can be some of the best sessions. I keep a running list of things I want to talk about with my therapist, so during weeks where there isn't a raging fire to put out, we can talk about ongoing maintenance issues.

As for Mr. Anxiety and Mr. Depression, I've come to understand that they will likely always be with me, but I can do certain things to avoid spontaneous visits and schedule our meetings a little more on my terms. Part of it is learning their likes and dislikes. For example, Mr. Anxiety loves travel, a third cup of coffee, and new business ventures. He tends to swing by when I'm hungover or will even get in bed with me in the middle of the night. Mr. Depression's interests include long, uninterrupted periods of very hard work without any breaks, listening to Jeff Buckley, watching airplane movies, and dabbling in agoraphobia. He likes to hang out with Ms. Period and usually hides when my friends are around.

Even more than knowing their hobbies and habits, though, knowing what Mr. Anxiety and Mr. Depression hate has become the key to my mental health. They both can't STAND exercise. Part of the reason I eat salad every day is because it makes them gag. And neither of them can read, so I always have multiple books going and it's the number one thing I reach for when either of them starts coming around.

Nevertheless, they will never leave me completely, and honestly, I'm okay with that. As I've said, I find growth during really tough times, and I know that Mr. Anxiety and Mr. Depression have also made me stronger, more empathetic, and more self-aware. I've even come to appreciate that chaotic bitch Ms. ADHD. I mean, my house is a mess and I have trouble finishing my own sentences because my brain is such a pinball machine, but I also know she has made me a ball of curiosity and I don't think I would have had such an interesting life without this disorganized clusterfuck of a brain.

> **THE SHIFT:** My mental health issues make life so hard → My mental health issues make me the unique person I am

I'm grateful to therapy for reframing my struggles as strengths. Just as the point of dating is not to get through it unscathed, the point of life is not to sail through without any scars (or at least some solid menty b's). We are human! We love imperfectly, we act irrationally, our brains are wonderful and awful—and I don't know why we ever try to pretend otherwise. (While I'm on the topic of mental health and dating crossover, therapy can also be a great place to talk about your love life. You don't always have to discuss Trauma with a capital T. Believe me, your therapist is down to figure out why Chris didn't call you back and help you break your unhealthy patterns around guys too!) And speaking of men and therapy, personally, I wouldn't date a guy who had never gone to therapy (and bonus points if he's still in it). I'm attracted to people who want to constantly improve themselves. Self-work is hot.

> **THE SHIFT:** Therapy is for people with problems → Therapy is for people who want the best for themselves

PARENTS ARE JUST PEOPLE:

HOW TO MAKE SENSE OF YOUR LIFE BY EXAMINING YOUR MOM AND DAD

"Children begin by loving their parents; as they grow
older they judge them; sometimes, they forgive them."

—Oscar Wilde, *The Picture of Dorian Gray*

For a while, I thought the main thing that defined me was the fact that I grew up in two different countries *hold for applause.* That was my "interesting" factor. And it was also where I could point to when looking for a place to blame all my toxic traits. I had to switch back and forth between using "fries" and "chips"—would you really be surprised if I ended up in rehab?!

However, I never had any negative feelings toward one place or the other—in fact, I was equally obsessed with the United States and the UK. I received a classic British education, and with it a sense of responsibility to be culturally aware—something that's stayed with me and evolved into a need to know everything about everyone. I was obsessed with reading Shakespeare and going to the theater after school. Kids in London have a lot of independence, and my friends and I could casually take the tube to see a show by ourselves, or head to Marks and Spencer for some fancy pesto pasta and pudding. I don't think I'll be that smart or worldly ever again.

Then every summer, I would go to Florida for two months to visit my grandparents, which felt like an exciting field trip to the epicenter of all things American: celebrity culture, huge parking lots, and suburban malls with Abercrombie and Limited Too (if you know, you know). I inhaled the exoticness of it and loved the juxtaposition of living in a chic, cosmopolitan city and then retreating to a comfortable, warm suburban town where I could wear a huge Bugs Bunny shirt and eat McDonald's.

I had to switch my accent to fit in with my British peers at school, and because I was only around my grandparents in Florida, I was forced to pick up a hobby and ended up a black belt in karate (weird flex but okay). But honestly, looking back now, I think the double life I led brought far more positives than negatives. These two cultures—refined British sophistication and brash, bold American outrageousness—have always lived in me and formed the core of who I am, and one might say they evolved into my personal brand of using expensive skin care products while digging into a rotisserie chicken barehanded. The duality of these perspectives (and the literal back-and-forth across the Atlantic) ignited an obsession with the different ways people can live, and how a place can shape your identity.

I always thought that the places I grew up in were the main thing that influenced me, for better or worse. And I suppose it could have stayed that way if I hadn't done the work to really examine the people who had schlepped me back and forth across the Atlantic and why they had done so.

This chapter is about self-discovery, but it's really about parent-discovery. *Because realizing that your parents are just regular, fucked-up people is an essential part of learning who you really are.* And realizing that they are the reason you are the specific brand of fucked-up that you are is another rite of passage altogether.

Here's my story: I grew up somewhat well-off in a posh neighborhood of London and went to private school. But I'm not a Kennedy. My parents are both self-made. They both grew up dirt-poor in the Midwest. My mom was the first person in her family to go to college. My dad's father grew up in a small, poor village in Lebanon with no running water. My dad used to get a can of Coke for his birthday each year. To get to a place where they were able to get married and go on vacations and send their kids to college, my parents had to work their asses off. I'm hugely proud of them and I think it's sad that they belong to a bygone era where you could actually level up based on merit. (At least for cisgendered white people—the system has always been rigged for Black, brown, queer, and disabled people, for whom it's not just a matter of putting in the work.) But for my parents at the time, their philosophy came down to three ideals:

1. Nothing is guaranteed.
2. Work till you die.
3. Take care of your family.

My dad has followed these principles to the extreme. He gets up at four o'clock every morning. He works like an animal and never takes a break. Seeing what he did for our family was debilitating as a young adult because it felt like, if he went from nothing to where he is now, and by the logic of immigrant mentality, I'm supposed to make even more of an up-ward leap—what the fuck am I supposed to do?!

Then I'd look to my mom, who was an equally daunting example but for different reasons. She had gone from an am-bitious young lawyer to meeting my dad and giving up her career. She wasn't that far along in her practice when she got pregnant with me, so it was more cost-effective to stay home and raise me. It was also just what was done at the time. My dad got a job in London so they packed up and moved, and suddenly she was unemployed, in a foreign country, changing diapers when she had thought she'd be making partner. She never talked about it when I was younger, but as an adult (and after prodding her relentlessly), I've been able to get a sense of the loss she felt on multiple levels. She made a sacrifice for her family that she thought was necessary at the time, but which carried into the rest of her life.

I guess you could say it carried into the rest of my life as well, because I live in fear of something like that happening to me. It's why I cut guys off if they don't confirm plans by one o'clock on the day of the date. I don't want to end up stuck, so instead I keep men at a distance. I saw how my mom's loss of individual identity resulted in her being consumed by motherhood, while my dad did what he thought he was sup-posed to do—work nonstop. He was always away on business, and we'd be lucky to see him occasionally right before bed. But it's not because he didn't care. It's because he wanted a different life for his kids from the one he'd busted his ass to escape. He was the kind of dad who instilled values above all else. He wanted us to have nice things. He wanted us to read voraciously. He wanted us to travel and experience the world.

Most of all, he wanted us to get good grades, work hard, and be successful. This also meant that when my brother or I did normal kid stuff, my parents came down on us so hard.

One day when I was fourteen, we had parent-teacher conferences. I was waiting for my mom in the car as she talked to my teachers, and when she came out . . . I'll never forget it because the woman who never, ever yelled got in the car and screamed at me. She was furious. She shrieked, "Christina! Your teachers are saying you're not paying attention, you're in your own world. You are at a private school in England! I want you to have everything I didn't have! I want you to have options. I want you to be happy. I want everything for you. And you're squandering it."

After that moment, I got my shit together. Because I finally understood the sacrifices she had made in order to give me what she hadn't been able to have. And while she wanted to instill in me a respect for education and a solid work ethic, what she really drilled into me was a responsibility to myself to choose the life that I want.

This has all made a lot more sense as I've examined my parents from a place of investigative self-work instead of just looking at how they serve me as parents. *Separating the "mom" and "dad" from the people who grew up and randomly ended up your parents is so incredibly important, and honestly I don't think you can really self-actualize until you've done it.* Looking at my parents through a different lens has allowed me to step into their shoes, seeing my dad as a crazed college student learning French and Arabic and working himself down to the bone, or imagining my mom walking the streets of London with a stroller and no friends within a thousand-mile radius. It's also helped me to understand myself more—why I became an English major (like my dad), and why I am so black-and-white when it comes to relationships (lawyer mentality).

It's made me realize that while I've empathized with my mom my entire life, I've also tried my hardest to avoid going down the same path that she did, to the point where I put guardrails up to protect my autonomy. It's why I've put so much into my friendships. And above all, into knowing what makes me happy. Because besides taking care of me and my brother, for a long time I wasn't sure what else made my mom happy. I know that having children can bring a sense of purpose to your life that is worth more than anything, but I also think you gotta know how to bring yourself joy. You can give everything you have to your family, but just make sure to save a little space for yourself.

Once my brother left for school, I really encouraged my mom to find something just for her. She joined an all women's running group. She made friends who boosted her up, she found solace and strength in the act of running, and she's been happier in these last ten years than I've ever seen her. The woman ran her first goddamned marathon at the age of fifty-five! Reclaiming her own life, embracing the ability to change, and being empowered by female friendships is what The Shift is all about. Seeing my mom live it out so beautifully in her own life has given me so much respect for her and made our relationship a million times stronger.

So, I highly recommend doing some digging into your own parents' lives. If you have a good relationship, ask them what their hardest moments in their twenties and thirties were. Ask them what they regret. Ask them how their life looks different from what they had imagined or dreamed for themselves. And try to listen, really listen, without thinking of them as your parent. I promise it will change your life.

THE SHIFT: My parents are ... my parents ⟶ Who could my parents have been if things had gone differently?

THE ULTIMATE SHIFT:

TAKING RESPONSIBILITY FOR YOUR OWN HAPPINESS

"Having fun is so fun."

—Tinx Original

There's a Goop article that changed my life. The gist of it is that happiness is a fleeting state. It's an abstract destination that we all strive to get to, but it's very hard to know when you've arrived and nearly impossible to maintain once you've gotten there. However, joy is a lot easier to recognize and far more attainable. Joy is in the little things. For me, it's driving to my favorite frozen yogurt place, getting my nails done in bright and outrageous designs, and spotting Broncos on the road (specifically baby-blue ones). None of these things has anything to do with long-term goals. They are tiny moments I can give myself. And when they are compounded, that is actually how I have found happiness.

I know I go on and on about knowing what makes you happy, but I'm really talking about knowing what brings you joy. Much of life is thinking of everything as a huge project, but the real stuff of life is in the mundane. So it is with joy. Start small. Make a playlist of all your favorite nineties songs. Drive an extra ten minutes to get a special latte, not just your regular iced coffee. Take a bath instead of a shower. It's not about figuring out what your career path looks like, or planning to move to a new city. *Don't make the key to your happiness something you can only have on vacation. Make it something you can get at the gas station.*

An important distinction here: The things that spark joy for you have got to be specific and unique. Can't be that you like music. Or tacos. Get more niche. Be a total freak like me and find absolute bliss in your favorite water bottle. Diet Coke in a glass bottle is another little thing that really does it for me. Trying new hot sauces too. I saw a blue Bronco this morning and I literally squealed like a child. Being delighted by these little things and appreciating the everyday is how I actually build a life that brings me pleasure.

Here's your assignment in two parts: First, find your blue Bronco. Perhaps it's seeing seagulls in parking lots. Or eating frozen grapes. Maybe resilient little three-legged dogs make you smile. Whatever your thing is, treat the world as a scavenger hunt and whenever you see something on your list, take it as a sign of good things coming your way. It's a little shot of joy, small on its own but something you can build up, brick by brick, until you suddenly have an abundance of things that bring you pure pleasure. Love what you love with abandon and make it something you can easily add into your day.

Okay, part two: Take what you love and make sure everyone else knows it too. Shout it from the rooftops. Because not only does it reinforce that positive connotation, injecting more power into each time you encounter it, but it also brings more of it into your world because the people you love start joining in the experience. For example, not only are blue Broncos my thing, but now I have everyone sending them to me. My friends text me when they find a really good hot sauce. The more you share the things you love, the more power you put behind them and the more you are able to collect back on them.

This is also a good barometer for relationships. Someone worth dating will also find joy in the things you love. When I think about the boyfriends who have loved me the most, they were also the ones the most on board with driving thirty minutes to get the best froyo. (And the one asshole who didn't? Should have dumped him way sooner than I did.) *Good guys are happy to see you happy.*

Same thing with friends. If you gave me ten bucks and told me to use it to make my friends happy, I'd be able to spend that money on very specific things depending on each friend. I know exactly what I'd get each person. Honestly, people who don't have strong and passionate interests make me uncomfortable. I guess it goes back to that whole fear-of-losing-yourself thing. I cling to the things that I love and make them my entire personality. Then I suddenly realize that happiness is actually all around me, it's just about the right framing. If done enough and made into a practice, it becomes your default state. So find whatever kooky things you enjoy and recklessly love the shit out them.

> **THE SHIFT:** Work toward a happy life ⟶ Build joy, brick by brick

DIFFERENT STROKES:
FOLLOWING YOUR OWN TIMELINE

"Follow your arrow wherever it points."

—Kacey Musgraves, "Follow Your Arrow"

I lost my virginity at nineteen. I became a TikToker at thirty. I am now in my early thirties, unmarried, with my nails painted like a fourteen-year-old. And I could not be happier with my life. That said, I spent the majority of my twenties feeling like I needed to catch up with some ambiguous idea of a grown-up, successful life. (Thankfully I didn't let that get in the way of my also living irresponsibly, traveling as much as I could, and jumping from random job to random job.)

I've said it before and I'll say it again: Your twenties are a mis-marketed decade. In movies and on TV we're fed this idea of our twenties being this incredible era—the time of our lives—when we are young and sexy and endlessly fun but also somehow rich and have everything figured out. And that could not be farther from the truth. Most of us spend our twenties not knowing what the fuck is going on and not really even knowing who we are. We put all this pressure on ourselves after watching movies where a girl moves to New York at the age of twenty-three and somehow has a job that you could only get if you have fifteen years of work experience. She lives in an apartment you could only get if you were a literal millionaire. She also meets the man of her dreams and lives happily ever after at an age when most of us are making forty-five thousand a year, living with three roommates, texting "Matt Tinder" to see if we left our sweatshirt at his place last night.

Even if your twenties are already in the rearview, you're still not out of the woods when it comes to timeline anxiety. In fact, the expectation of marriage and babies doubles down on the calculations, turning us into sad little mathematicians figuring out that by the time we meet someone, date seriously, get engaged, get married, get pregnant, and have 2.5 kids, we will be approximately the age of a typical grandmother. Every family gathering is basically a gauntlet of relatives asking "Have you met anyone yet?" or "When are you going to settle down?" like it's something that could have possibly slipped your mind.

I wish I would have seen my twenties as a time of learning and known that thirties are when you really start to build a life. And I wish that I could have told my twenty-three-year-old self to be more present and keep my sights set on my own path, instead of constantly comparing my situation to everyone else's.

I think the number one thing I repeat more than any other bit of advice is that comparison is the thief of joy. And the root cause of most of the stress and anxiety that women seek out my guidance for comes down to feeling like you should be at a certain point in your life by a specific age.

Here's the thing: The majority of the pressure that we all feel is pressure we put entirely on ourselves. Which also means it's ultimately under our control. The thoughts you tell yourself become the reality that you live in, and guess what? *Timelines are completely made up.* (And usually based on what people did like three generations earlier. So fuck 'em.)

Timelines are harmful and counterproductive to self-growth and finding true love. Think of it this way—what's added pressure going to do? It's not going to accomplish anything besides making you more stressed out. So ground yourself in the present day of your amazing life. Imagine that a year from now all the things you covet will be yours, so how do you want to spend your days in the meantime? *Have fun, make memories, and live as if the odds are in your favor.*

If your friends are at different points in life and it makes you feel a bit insecure in comparison, switch that thought from a place of scarcity mindset to the realization that if it can happen for them, it can happen for you. Just be there for them. Acknowledge that you are in different places (I'm sure they've noticed as well). And make it fun instead of awkward. I guarantee your friends with newborn babies would love to hear about your crazy date as they sit there breastfeeding. Also, you will reap the benefits when it's your turn to have kids and your friends have figured out all the hard stuff for you. It's actually a really beautiful thing to be in different stages and still be able to support each other. Friendship isn't about being in the same exact places in life, it's about being there for your friends no matter what stage they're in.

THE SHIFT: I need to figure out my life before it's too late
→ Before it's too late for what? Is there an asteroid heading toward Earth? Are you going to turn into a pumpkin at midnight? Please don't waste precious moments of your youth that you will not be able to get back!

AFTERWORD

Throughout the process of writing this book, I was single, but then I met someone. I had dubbed 2022 "the Summer of Getting Outside" and scheduled a bunch of trips with friends and decided to just have fun. I was hungover at a party, barefoot and barely wearing makeup, acting like a lunatic. Within days, this guy had booked a cross-country flight to stay with me at my house.*

There are a lot of guidelines in this book, and as a suddenly not-so-single person I realized that dammit, now I needed to practice what I preach. In that delirious love-drunk state of a new relationship, I had to double down on all the advice I give to others. I needed to be vigilant about nourishing my friendships even in the middle of the gooey part of early dating where you just want to wrap yourself around the other person and spend every second with them. I needed to avoid putting him on a pedestal, make sure to carve out time for myself and my work, and remember that I'm on my own timeline.

But in the midst of taking a taste of my own medicine, it became clear that there is one thing that outdoes every concept in this book: following your own happiness. Regardless

---

* Box Theory, anyone?

of what happens with this guy or any guy that follows, I am the source of my happiness, and that is how I know I will be good no matter what. When you are doing you, no amount of strategizing or theorizing can outdo the power of knowing what gives you joy and throwing yourself headfirst into it. We forget that "happily ever after" can be a thing you give yourself, and then choose to spend with someone else.

I hope this book has helped you. I hope you are able to practice The Shift in small moments throughout your day and never forget how important your relationship with yourself is. If you ever get off track, stuck in scarcity mindset, playing a side character instead of the main character, just connect back with a little happiness trigger that's only for you. Keep building that joy brick by brick.

Perhaps most important, keep taking care of each other. As my bestie Camilla says, your female friendships are the through line in your life. Date and love with abandon, but don't forget to love your girlfriends just as deeply. They are the real prize.

Last but not least, I love you. I really do. I wish I could create a commune where all of us could hang out and eat snacks and tell embarrassing stories. In the meantime, I will keep sharing every detail of my life with you guys, and thank you for allowing me the honor of doing so.

TINX'S GLOSSARY

bajiggity: As seen in the movie *The Sweetest Thing*, a state of being emotionally and/or sexually worked up over a man; acting weird over a guy.

Box Theory: A dating philosophy that explains how men put women into one of three boxes upon meeting them (date, hookup, friend).

Boyfriend Sickness: A mild-to-serious condition affecting girls with boyfriends; symptoms include choosing boyfriend over friends and losing yourself in a relationship.

breakup antibodies: A substance produced in the body after a breakup that strengthens your immune system to protect against future heartbreaks.

car time: Time spent in the car; sacred space.

crush list: One part organization, one part manifestation. This is a list you should keep refreshed at all times to track strangers, friends, celebrities, and any guys who make your fanny flutter. Do not underestimate the power of the crush list to call that energy into your life.

ESWB: Emotional Support Water Bottle, a reusable water bottle that can provide hydration and comfort during Rich Mom Walks, therapy sessions, car time, or any work being done on a laptop.

holding a funeral: A process in which you let go of a fuckboi or dude you never dated. Light some candles. Put on some Jeff Buckley. Drink a glass of wine and set that motherfucker free.

leg on wall: A therapeutic form of restorative movement, done by lying on the ground and placing legs vertically in the air against the wall, best performed with girlfriends. I am not a doctor but doing this thirty minutes a day has changed my life.

menty b: A mental breakdown that occurs on a seasonal basis, while traveling, or before a menstrual cycle.

phone level: A barometer of TV show/movie interest level on a scale of 1 (not looking at the phone once, completely riveted) to 10 (scrolling on phone the entire time).

Reverse Box Theory: A phenomenon in which a woman puts a man in the dating box before even meeting him, thereby elevating him to an unrealistic and unearned level of importance.

Rich Mom Energy: People or things can have RME. Saying fuck it and cooking yourself a really delicious steak on a Wednesday night and watching Bravo for three hours is RME. Buying yourself a gift when you get a promotion is RME. You don't have to be rich or be a mom. It's a vibe you create through advocating for yourself.

Rich Mom Walk: A walk one goes on (preferably daily, and in the morning) to clear the mind. Can be on a treadmill if needed. Can be with a friend or solo. Music/podcast/audiobook and Bala Bangles are optional. Coffee is mandatory. It's a reminder to take even just ten minutes out of your day for yourself. Think positively and hype yourself up. Let the movement and fresh air heal whatever's troubling you. Manifest what you want for the day.

The Scent: An energy level and/or essence that is projected when a woman is actively dating and therefore, her dates beget more dates; i.e., "That date sucked but at least now I have The Scent on me."

shmangalanging: The best activity on earth.

Shovel Gang: A group of people who participate in the act of eating salad with a spoon.

wobbly: When you're on the verge of a menty b.

RECOMMENDED READING

MEMOIRS
- *Inside Out* by Demi Moore
- *The Woman I Wanted to Be* by Diane von Furstenberg
- *Blowing My Way to the Top* by Jen Atkin
- *The Vanity Fair Diaries* by Tina Brown
- *Every Day I'm Hustling* by Vivica A. Fox

ESSAYS
- *Trick Mirror* by Jia Tolentino
- *We're Going to Need More Wine* and *You Got Anything Stronger?* by Gabrielle Union
- *I Feel Bad About My Neck* by Nora Ephron
- *Untamed* by Glennon Doyle
- *The Wreckage of My Presence* by Casey Wilson
- *Tiny Beautiful Things* by Cheryl Strayed

ACKNOWLEDGMENTS

I'd like to thank my mom. Mom, I wouldn't be who I am without you. You saw my potential and through love and determination pushed me to be better. You always believed in me no matter what. No matter how many times I faltered you always cheered from the sidelines. You made me strong and ambitious. I love you forever. I'd also like to thank my dad. Thank you for pushing me. Thank you for working so hard and for giving me a better life than you had. Thank you for always picking up the phone in the middle of the night and calming me down when I'm scared. Thank you to my little brother, JM. You are my favorite person on earth, and I would die without you. See, I can be dramatic because you are not. Thank you for making me laugh harder than any other person, and for being the voice of reason and balance. It's us till the end. Thank you to my grandparents for showing me a different kind of love, a gentle love that I needed so much. Thank you for working so hard to give us all a better shot. Thank you to Aunt Paula and Uncle Steve for making me feel special and loved and safe.

Thank you to my best friends who I am in awe of. Brian, thank you for everything. I truly mean everything. Casey, thank you for being the best roommate a girl could ever ask for. Thank you for the comfort and security. To Abigail and Molly, thank you for the softest landing into the real world.

I will think about the purple palace forever. Dickie, thanks for being my dick. Vee, Haley, Momo, thank you for showing me what pure love is in friendship and for some of the happiest memories of my life. Katherine and Iman, thank you for the enduring love and companionship. To Jyoti, for being my first, truest best friend and my forever inspiration. You shaped me. To Camilla for all of the trips, all of the texts, all of the endless conversations, and all of our deep shared thoughts. To Reidie for being Big Sissy. To Daisy, Chloe, and Ashley for the fun, the orange wine, and the never-ending Sundays. To Greg for being my mentor and friend. For being a rock. To Neil for giving me space to be creative and for all the gentle sweetness. To Wig for the loyalty and laughs. To Jesse for being weird with me. To Lucas. For one of the most beautiful friendships I have ever experienced. For consistency. For hiking club.

Thank you to my team: Sethy, for finding me and believing in me and taking a risk on the oldest influencer ever. Thank you for being crazy with me. Thank you for never faltering. Thank you for the endless, genuine kindness and love that is in every cell of your being. To Saba, my baby and also my mother. What would I do without you, Jamie, I just don't know. To Lauren, my cocaptain. Viche's other mom. My buddy in everything. To Hailey for being a bubbly warm light. And for making me look beautiful, even when I have drunk three bottles of wine the night before.

To Pilar and Byrd. For understanding me intuitively from the moment we met. For being so unbelievably on top of it. For being professional and getting it done and being smart. To Caroline and Alec. For slaying through sunny and stormy seas.

Thank you to Hilary for being Hilary. I liked you the second we met. Thank you for your smarts and wit and complexity and compassion. Thank you. I'm gonna make it all worth it.

Thank you to the team at Simon & Schuster for giving me the opportunity and allowing me to fulfill a lifelong dream.

Thank you to Allison. I think you're the coolest person I've ever met and I don't care if that's not allowed. I would be dead without you. I hope you come to my wedding.

Thank you to every boy who ever ghosted me. I'm serious, thank you. Everything is copy.

And finally to all of you. Thank you to my community who I live for. Thank you for every question, every DM, every phone call into my radio show. Thank you for letting me into your lives and trusting me. I hope this helps.

INDEX

ABOUT THE AUTHOR

CHRISTINA NAJJAR, popularly known as Tinx, is a digital creator, advice expert, podcast host, and *New York Times* bestselling author. Tinx's wit and candor have established her as a resounding voice for women, with her uniquely engaging and empathetic approach to content resonating with millions. From her satirical "Rich Mom" content and takes on pop culture to her theories on sex, dating, and relationships and her honest reviews and recommendations of everything from food and restaurants to beauty, fashion, and lifestyle products, Tinx possesses an effortless ability to capture the cultural zeitgeist. She has developed a devoted fan base of those who come for her expert advice (which is often given with her famous mini mic in hand) and to have a great laugh at the same time. In 2022, Tinx launched her podcast and live call-in radio show with SiriusXM, *It's Me, Tinx*, sharing everything her followers have come to know and love about her content while offering an intimate glimpse into her life. Tinx's undeniable impact on social media earned her the distinction of one of *Forbes*'s Top Creators of 2022 and again in 2023.